I0883290

LANDFALL 239

May 2020

Editor Emma Neale
Founding Editor Charles Brasch (1909–1973)

Cover: Star Gossage, *I have sung my way through this world*, 2018, oil on canvas, 1015 x 1015mm. Collection Auckland Art Gallery Toi o Tāmaki

Published with the assistance of Creative New Zealand.

creative nz
Arts Council of New Zealand *Toi Aotearoa*

OTAGO UNIVERSITY PRESS

CONTENTS

THE LANDFALL REVIEW

EMMA NEALE

Charles Brasch Young Writers' Essay Competition 2020 Judge's Report

From formal academic essays exploring the benefits of early childhood education or the socio-historical changes in depictions of disabled people; to a personal essay about a grandfather's escape from Nazi-occupied Lithuania; to a strong argument about identity as a fourth-generation Chinese New Zealander; to an astonishingly calm and philosophical enumeration of the changes witnessed by a sixteen-year-old resident of Christchurch; and to a lyrical, sensuous, song-like study of the place of the pomegranate in myth and art, the essays entered for the 2020 Charles Brasch Young Writers' Essay Competition took me well beyond the cloister of my study. Each night when I talked to my family about what I'd been doing that day, I felt like I had the tales of a traveller who'd broken all the limitations of the Covid-19 lockdown.

How do you separate out one potent impression from another in a diverse field? I looked for essays that achieved the synchronicity and smoothness of style and subject gliding together—like a clean pairs-lift in ice-skating, perhaps. Sometimes the young writers tackled worthy content but in a heavily formal, recondite style that strained for seriousness through a fog of abstractions. In other instances, competent writers marshalled the facts but their writing lacked a burning sense of conviction, or a striking originality of style, a fresh angle on a perennial problem, or it gave in to cliché. Other essays were so heavily encrusted with simile and metaphor that they were like a monarch wearing all their regalia and jewellery at once. The progress of any argument was dragged down by furs, chains, rings and crowns, its joints and spine cracking and the whole show toppling under the strain.

The most gripping essays have motion; they develop or travel somewhere. Sure, they might only end in a tentative arrival, or the track might go full circle, but even a circular walk can be enlivened with observations of a flickering or altering perception. Many of the young writers who entered I think could ask themselves, does this essay chart a change of some kind—historical, social, internal? Have I sharpened the reader's understanding of that shift?

Two essays are **highly commended** this year. They are 'The Air Which Surrounds the Bridge' by **Xiaole Zhan**, and 'Mr Fox and Me' by **David Simes**.

Third place goes to **Shanti Mathias** for 'The Starfish Method', a strong, supple and bold examination of a father–daughter coach–athlete relationship striated with love and pressure to achieve.

Second place goes to **Lily Holloway** for 'Waiting for Metamorphosis', in which a young writer looks to Ovid's myths for language and experience to help her to articulate the grief, pain, confusion and fear that follow a sexual assault. While seeking illumination from myths in which women are brutally silenced or transformed into animals is fraught and indeed possibly retraumatising, this young writer bravely reorients herself sexually and emotionally, carefully analysing her own responses both to mythic patterns and gradually adjusted medication.

First place goes to **Grace Lee** for 'Body/Love'. To be self-expository and blunt, part of me didn't want this essay to win. When I realised what the topic was, I flinched as from a hot poker. The writer tackles anorexia, a condition I had as a late teenager and have only ever managed to write about glancingly, perhaps once or twice, now that I'm deep into middle age. The topic stirs up painful and incoherent sediment about family, femininity, personal expectations, and the cryptically intersecting gridlines of genetics, experience and culture in personality. I dreaded reading something that aestheticised the appearance and mindset of the anorexic adolescent.

This essay subtextually acknowledges those dangers and is deft, elegant, intelligent. Using a sophisticated language and a light touch, it reaches out beyond the sharply rendered personal experience into discussion of pop and canonical identities (David Bowie and John Keats) and finally to a more healthily distanced, analytical understanding of what the illness has been 'about' for the writer—a bid for self-reliance, an impulse to attain perfection—and to an understanding of how much that urge has sacrificed.

GRACE LEE

Body/Love

All the long raw days of my starving I felt myself shrivel into dust and flower into bone. I half-fed myself on chemical dregs. The scales slipped down into numbers I hadn't seen since I was a child; and I, precariously walking the wire of my obsession, relished it. I swallowed whole the tyrannical myth of cleanness: a body with not a wisp of excess, not an inch nor a gram to spare; a perfect closed system with no miscellaneous slop of food intruding upon it. My ascetic aesthetic. The bones of my shoulders flaring like dead coral.

My imagination dried into a goose-step of numbers and lists and merciless arithmetic. I wandered exhausted and half-crazed through crowded streets, barely seen, barely seeing. I turned myself inward into my desperate death-drive and spoke to no one. I read nothing, wrote less. Every night until the first acid streak of dawn I lay awake, bruises blooming on my hipbones, overworked heart kicking like mad. In some way I was less woman than I was a burning brand of single-minded discipline, a pillar of twisting agon, an island, a pearl.

I would have told you then, without a trace of irony, that the most beautiful woman in the world was one of Giacometti's. How fiercely lovely to become a blade-thin slash in the air, to defy the very concept of dimensionality. I revelled in various sources of exceptionality, of removal from the world: can't buy clothes off the rack, can't donate blood; don't need tampons or bras or washing-up liquid; for some reason, never felt thirsty. I indulged myself in a fantasy of self-sufficiency wherein I floated vaguely above ground level, an increasingly untethered balloon inflated by diet soda, completely contained, a world unto myself. My world exploded into warfare every time I walked past a bakery cabinet. Every half-kilogram lost was an international event.

There is only so much, however, that a system can contain. My body burned away from outside in. My madness and hunger and mania swelled wildly from inside out. One rainy June morning, waiting for a delayed train in Leamington Spa, I gave up. I bought millionaire's shortbread from the beautiful elfin blonde girl at the platform café and waited for the sky to fall and the seven trumpets to sound. This failed to happen. The train arrived and the Midlands trundled past, a soaked greyish sponge. In a sudden moment of depressing clarity I realised that all my elaborately theorised self-fashioning project had really made me was *hungry*.

Admitting you want to be alive sans weight-based provisos is hard. Starting to eat, from the first time my mother fed me solids to the dozens of times I've subsequently reintroduced myself to the concept of a full stomach, is hard. It opens up a whole new category of experience, not all of it pleasant. Nothing worse in early days than feeling like an overstuffed taxidermy specimen, convinced that everyone on the street can see you bursting at the seams, watching the hours drip away too fast before you have to eat again. But of course you *want* to eat. All the cravings of the last several weeks and months confront you at once in their monstrous metastasis. Eating like you'll never get to eat again, stretch marks spreading over your stomach. Pretending you don't see the terrain of sharp bones softening in the mirror. So squirmingly uncomfortable in your body that you could scream when someone brushes against you in a crowd.

Berlin, c.1976: David Bowie is floating back to earth, shedding the rail-thin brittle beauty of his legendary LA coke-fiend days. They say there was a madly driven genius. There was a flamboyantly dressed skeleton being spoon-fed ice cream by his managers. There was 'Station to Station', its spectacularly weird associative universe, its private language of artfulness that unravels into wilful obscurity. Its pitch of otherworldly bliss, building slowly through a gloriously stagey five(!)-minute-long intro until it explodes into rapturous triplets, sending bursts of startled birds fluttering off a landscape that heaves itself into mountains: 'once I could never be down'. But feel the strain in that optimism, the half-sob in 'searching', the loneliness of 'once' fighting the unboundedness of 'never'. What's infinity, what's eternal flight, if it can be contained in that temporal deixis? If he scraped the edge of heaven, but only once, only back then?

And so, Berlin: the flannel shirts, the dirty-blond hair, the shadowboxing. A vocabulary built from scratch. First, nothing at all, the soundtrack to a Martian landscape put through a synthesiser. And then little words, tentative in their uncomfortable sincerity, leaving behind wildly unspooling visions of rapture to find an unblinking even-handedness. We can be heroes, just for one day. Two steps forward and one back, grandeur checked by provisionality; it carries in its construction the knowledge of the temporary, contingent thing that is man. It begins with him driving manic circles around parking lots, suddenly terrified of the silence. It begins with him raiding Iggy Pop's refrigerator for fine cheeses. It begins with meat-and-two-veg pub meals and doing his own grocery shopping.

Eating incurs the need to develop auxiliary skills. That of sitting with people three times a day to dine and, necessarily, to talk. Of navigating again the various practicalities of feeding yourself: comparing prices of different oatmeal brands, diplomatically negotiating a shared pizza's toppings, thinking about whether one mylk is more ethical than another (or, indeed, than milk), defending your cookware in a shared kitchen, remembering when and how you're supposed to elegantly pick up a bill. Living in the world, a world of shared, performative, social, un/ethical consumption, is so much more complicated and surprising than living in the stifling majesty of your own mind.

Katy Waldman writes about snacking while working: a cherished messy synthesis, popcorn and chocolate going in, words coming out.[1] The give-and-take of simultaneously absorbing and putting out, of opening yourself up to the world. Something beautiful about it, cracker crumbs on a keyboard, voracious and prolific. John Keats subconsciously knew this, or something like it—that is, the real Keats, not the sickly half-blown creature reverse-engineered from his death but a young man untroubled by doom, hungry, ambitious, sexual. He wrote about wine, cheap theatres, ripe nectarines, a juicy cut of beef. La Belle Dame and her 'roots of relish sweet'—well, nothing more mercilessly seductive than a fresh radish.[2]

Perhaps in another, longer, life he could have been a great food writer. Not a fragile consumptive, not being consumed but restlessly consuming. Savouring pheasants, claret, translations of Homer; 'candied apple, quince, and plum'; his lover's 'million-pleasured breast'.[3] The way to the poet's other world is not over but through this one. Cold wine, a bursting ripe strawberry, the nightingale's song that fills him up bodily and soaks into him until he and the lush wild world are one.

Perhaps in place of my fantasy of self-sufficiency, my belief that my body could be a perfect system, a beautiful miniature in pristinely turned bone, I might be able to love my mess, the astonishing grace of an unequal give-and-take; imbalance, asymmetry, offering without expectation. All the ways I have come face to face with the world without tallying inputs and outputs. Everything I've given without stint, and everything I have been given. The people who have looked out for me, cooked brunch for me when I'm hung over, fallen asleep curled up with me thousands of miles from home, absorbed the worst things I've done and told me that they still loved me, bought me lunch, waited up for me, held my hand on a steep downhill, sent me a message out of the blue, seen me off at airports, loved me without wanting anything back.

I want to absorb a model of the world that's awake to the irreducible surplus of phenomenal experience. An astonishingly, cartoonishly perfect apple in a market in Copenhagen. A baby smiling at me through the gap between bus seats. The monk who stopped me on a bright winter morning to give me a set of prayer beads. Watching two baristas chasing a car out of a drive-thru in pouring rain, both in fits of laughter, bearing a corrected order under an apron with exaggerated care.

It seems unthinkably naive to go through the world thinking that there is any such thing as a true gift, or an act of grace, or an inexplicable phenomenon. Everyone is supposed to be more or less predictable along the lines of their self-interest, each place more or less similar to another, every possible occurrence reducible to its place in the filing cabinet of human experience. But maybe we're not doomed to always think that way. Maybe I can take in without incurring a debt. Maybe I can love without wanting. Maybe there's more in the world than any system can contain.

NOTES

1 www.slate.com/articles/double_x/cover_story/2015/12/we_need_to_reject_the_false_narratives_around_anorexia.html

2 John Keats, 'La Belle Dame Sans Merci'.

3 Homer, 'The Eve of St. Agnes', XXX.4; Keats, 'To Fanny'.

CAROLYN GILLUM

A Good Dog

Dog is mute, and so am I today. At Mme Juliette's he sits on the chair beside me and we take turns to lap from the bowl of water I place there, then we hang out our tongues to dry like soft flags.

When Mme Juliette arrives to take our order I retrieve my tongue and mime like *I want a cup of coffee so big I'll never want again*. I saw my father do this once, through the window of his vast office, stuffed with mahogany furniture like too many teeth. He mimed it at the woman who sat outside his door and organised his life and when she saw him her whole face transformed, like she loved him or something, and she laughed like crazy.

Mme Juliette does not laugh. She tilts her head like a blackbird and notes things in her little notebook, and later I get served whatever my father's men-in-black decide. Usually, it's some cat-shit like decaf Americano, because apparently there's this thing inside me no one can risk unleashing, particularly—especially—in public. Despite my father's view that the General Public are pig-ignorant.

Sometimes I wonder if Mme Juliette thinks the same. You know, that the people in this country—who live so far from France, who are such arse-licking Francophiles—don't even realise her accent is fake.

The thing is, though—and I told my father this—pigs are actually quite smart. His brow shifted then, and a skin roll closed over his eyes, shrinking his pupils, giving him this zombie gaze he's famous for—well, among people who don't respect his genius. He spoke without looking at me, which is how you know you've approached the line that is not to be crossed, and said it's possible to be both pig-ignorant and smart, and cited my sister as an example.

But Sophie ... man. She's like an exploding Lichtenstein painting. She only wears red, blue and yellow. She paints her eyelids gold, her lips black. It makes her eyes blaze like the flames in Bunsen burners. I visited her in Paris during the summer, back when it was possible for me to travel further than

Mme Juliette's café, which is how I know a French accent from a fake.

That summer was hot. The beige Paris streets were hazy with heat and it was like watching the world through spliffed eyes, although mostly we only got stoned on Saturdays. Then we'd go to Le Pound with her friends, neck pills and dance all night like somehow the world was just gonna keep on turning.

I pretend to laugh when Sophie mocks our dad. But when she does Father Zombie I get this hook in my stomach. It seizes at me, clenching like Morse code: *traitor, traitor*. In Paris I used to tug at the ties of my bandana and check behind me, as if my father might be lurking there with his entourage. Lol. Like anyone in France would even know who he was.

Sophie caught me once, the weight of her damp arm falling on my shoulders. She rubbed my head like I was some kind of puppy, which I pretended not to like. *When are you going to realise, little brother?*

Good question, Soph.

Good Dog. That's what she called her exhibition. I was pretty amped for it; I thought it'd be some kind of homage to Dog because he's always been pretty special to her. But it turned out to be these random shots of Sophie wearing only headphones, investigating her shit under a microscope. When I say shit, I mean like actual, like the stuff that comes out your arse. Her arse. There were macro photos of these turds squashed between glass slides, over which she'd drawn these childish happy dog faces. In some she'd even glued old photos of Dog smiling, his tongue hanging out.

I recognised the headphones. She'd starting wearing them around our house before she moved to Paris. They look like the clip-on Princess Leia coils she'd had as a kid. *To block out the noise of our family shit, she said.*

I said the exhibition was super wild, but I don't know why she made something so ugly. Who'd want to look at that? My father didn't say anything when he saw the photos. He just dropped them on the bench where he used to chuck Dog's lead. They lay there until my mother scooped them into the shredder. Sophie doesn't use our last name for her art. Maybe that's why my parents don't cut her off. Financially, I mean.

Mme Juliette is older than me, maybe even older than thirty. I tried to mime a question about her age once and she thought I was ordering for my whole security detail and it got really fucking complicated. This little twitch started on her forehead and it reminded me of my father, which made me tense, and my bandana slipped over my eyes like a blindfold because I started to sweat, so I stick to what's expected now. I want to make the right impression.

But Mme Juliette's eyes ... man, they're like ponds. Pale green like the pool in the forest I imagined at school when we did that test—the one that's meant to reveal your personality. All my friends imagined some beach where girls with tanned breasts bounced up and down with a volleyball; all while I was slinking into this silky water. When it closed over me it was like I'd never even existed.

Mme Juliette's eyes are especially bright against her black-and-white-striped T-shirt. I sometimes wonder if I like her because she looks like a prisoner too. But mostly I like the way she looks at me when I make my order. I like the way she listens, how she thumbs that little notebook into that perfect-sized pocket in her apron. I want to be that notebook, I want to press against her leg as she foams the milk.

I'm not mute, not like Dog. But if he can't talk, why should I? Talking out of turn is what got us where we are. And I can still use my voice. I can bark, for example. Sometimes at the dinner table I just bark at Dog, so he knows I'm thinking of him. I like him to know I'm here, listening, because it can be very lonely not being able to communicate what you want.

After my father's resignation I spent a long time alone in my parents' home. It's pretty big, their house, guarded by the men-in-black whose hips are bulked with intentionally ill-concealed weapons. They circle the property like poachers and size me up in their telescopic lenses, like I'm an animal they'd enjoy shooting. During this period I made a study of dog noises and built up quite a repertoire. Sometimes when I walk around our property I try them out—a yip then a yowl, a long howl, then a series of back-off barks. You should hear the neighbourhood dogs when I get going. It's very satisfying.

Dog lost his voice thanks to our neighbours, and since this is the subject that can unleash that thing inside me, I'll just say they called noise control and leave it at that.

But they called like every fucking day. They even started a petition. Can you believe it? Dog made too much noise, they said. All the time. We live in the kind of street where people launch a petition if you fart. Anyway, someone released it to the media, where it was covered by all the newspapers. *Is nothing sacred?* my mother said, dropping the paper onto the bench as if it were a turd.

At the time my father was a well-known man, so he had to be seen to act. The problem was, I'd gone to Fiji when it all kicked off, and I was pretty focused on the problem I had there. Specifically, I was focused on how my father was going to react when he found out about the problem I had there. I mean, he knew I'd hired the resort. He knew about the party. But he did not know about the rows and rows of white lines, or the way they reflected into infinity in that mirror.

But you should've seen him. He was a fucking hero. He flew over to Fiji as soon as he heard, walked in all quiet and in control, and people just jumped to. Boom, two days later we were home.

Sometimes I lie on my bed and imagine how it must feel to be able to act like that, to just *do* what needs to be done. To live with such solidity and certainty. I cannot think of a single place inside myself that would support the weight of that kind of confidence.

A couple of months later my father had to resign. The General Public were pretty upset because they loved him. But my father was right about how pig-ignorant they are, because they just accepted his story: that he wanted to spend more time at home with us, right at the peak of his career. But then I believed it too. Right up until the moment he said he'd rather gouge his eyes out than spend any more time with a fuck-up like me.

On the day of his resignation I was riding home from the press conference alone in the back of his big black car, the one that rolls like a hearse, when I saw Mme Juliette's café. All those little red, white and blue flags dancing and snapping in the breeze. I jumped out at the lights and when I pushed open the door an old-fashioned bell jangled. Mme Juliette looked up from where she was talking in French to another woman, and when she smiled I wanted to lie down and beg.

Hey, I said, hitching the back of my shorts as I crossed the floor. Her friend whispered my father's name and her smile froze. But she got the beans grinding and the steam busting out the machine and served me an actual cappuccino like I asked for, with real caffeinated coffee and a decent layer of foamed milk. She handled the éclair so tenderly, like a tiny puppy. She placed it on a delicate white napkin in the centre of the plate. She didn't say a word, even when security arrived.

I like the word leaked. Sophie likes it too. I like how it implies you could not hold it in. You are not to blame, you could not help it. It makes me think of abdication, a word I only learned recently, but apparently it's something I'm good at vis-à-vis responsibility.

Someone leaked something about the Fiji debacle. And someone else, a woman from the media—*a vampirous little whore*, my father said—started investigating. It turned out it would have been a pretty big deal for a person of my father's standing to be implicated in the 'alleged bribery and coercion of foreign officials to protect his son'.

My memories of the Fiji party are as hazy as those Paris streets, but sometimes the remembering happens—on that 3am carousel, an endless projection of shameful images burning the backs of my eyes. Dog senses this and he crawls closer to me in bed. He lets me hug him like my dad hugged me when I broke a window with my drone, when he laughed and ruffled my hair and said, *No worries, son, easily fixed.*

When my father resigned, he posed with me for TV crews and newspaper photographers. I used to work out a lot so I wore a singlet and matching shiny blue jogging shorts. I oiled my biceps so they'd glisten under the lights, and flexed them like I was just off to the gym, keeping lean and mean, like that's the sort of thing me and my dad might do together now we had so much time to spend with each other.

I was sad, I said to the cameras. I told them how upset I was that he'd resigned, which was only twenty percent true. My father had been more upset than I thought about quitting—so that's the truth of my sadness. Really though, I was looking forward to hanging with him. I said what a great role model and awesome dad he was. That was one hundred percent truth.

My father said I'd been very supportive, and he put his arm around my shoulders and squeezed me close, in a fatherly, manly way, and we beamed at the cameras, father and son together. Flash, flash flash. After the cameras were lowered, he dug his fingers into my shoulder so hard I thought he'd break through my skin. *Wtf?* I thought. But I knew he didn't mean to hurt me.

He dropped his hand and strode after a journalist, slipping his arm around her shoulder until she ducked away. The next day I could see five purple circles on my skin, one for each finger and thumb.

The day after my father resigned he took Dog out with him first thing in the morning and returned alone. I remember howling. I remember how soft his chest felt under my palms, how wide his zombie eyes became as he fell, and that blank moment before pain blew open the side of my head.

I remember him cradling his fist. I remember crying like a girl as the men-in-black carried me away like I was already fucking dead.

A few days after that Dog came back. He appeared in my bedroom one night, exactly as if he'd never left, shaking his black curly head. He crawled into my bed and licked my face and nestled his hot furry body against mine.

When Dog and I walk home from Mme Juliette's, the men-in-black follow as usual in their jeep. You can't even take a shit around here without one of them hovering. Once I did pull down my pants and open my anus in the middle of the road. They had me bundled in the back seat faster than they can yell one of their facile insults.

Today Dog and I pretend to chase them into our drive while I bark at them. The one who guards the gates gives me a look. He usually calls me something that refers to women's genitalia, which if I weren't being mute I'd say, *à la* Sophie, that it's a fucking compliment to be compared to a vulva.

No one is home. My mother and father used to be here all the time, but sometimes I wonder if they even live here any more. Maybe they just moved away without me. I get a bowl from the cupboard and go to my room. I can't lock it because I can't close the door. My father removed the handle. There's a rough hole where it used to be, and on bad days I run my finger around the inside and drive all the little splinters into my skin.

I bought some treats for Dog from the shop next to Mme Juliette's, which I purchased using the art of mime. I'm pretty good at it now. I cup my hands near my face and bark, sharp and loud like Dog used to, and I munch at the invisible food in my palms, I really project the snuffling, let the saliva dribble from my jowls over my fingers.

The man behind the counter was wearing a magenta turban and his forehead was furrowed with folds so deep I wanted to crawl into the cocoon between them. Eventually he caught the eye of one of the black-clothed men behind me and went to the shelf without a word, returning with a bag of Good Dog Temptations.

Dog and I sit on my bed and I pour the Temptations into a bowl between us. We eat our biscuits in the usual silence, then I lie back with my head on the pillow. I'm not allowed the internet, so I don't have a phone or a computer. These days I just close my eyes if I want to watch my favourite movie.

I'm arriving at Mme Juliette's. I work there now, although today is my day off. I've come in to see her because she's my girlfriend. She waves when I open the door, throwing me that beautiful smile, and now I have time to catch it, let it soar inside me.

Mme Juliette makes me a proper cappuccino, like the one she made the day my dad resigned. She draws a chocolate heart in foam so thick I could sleep forever under its blanket. Later she joins us outside. Her blue scarf has a splatter of icing sugar on it. On the table she sets down water for Dog, and a chocolate éclair she's cut into three equal portions.

Woof, I say.

She smiles.

When we're finished eating she ruffles my hair and kisses my cheek. *You're a good dog*, she says, in an accent I realise is real.

CLAIRE LACEY

hippocampus

sea-horse. XVI—L. Gr. kámpos sea-monster

Tail curls around kelp
locks tight
against tidepull.

We don't swim well
that's the joke
Poseidon's steeds shrunk
to centimetres:
elegant, delicate, slow

and so adapted to anchor
each eye independent
like a chameleon's

to watch a wide periphery
see danger approaching
from two directions
at speed that exceeds escape.

We wait to be prey
to the grasping crabclaw
or a current that shakes
us loose, sweeps us to shore
to choke and desiccate.

We envy the loch horse,
large and lethal,

which drags unsuspecting women
below the waterline
and devours them.

We wish to be so ungentled.
Nervy and shy, wide-eyed
and snorting, caught between
flight and freeze, reduced
to hope that today is
your turn, not mine.

JOHANNA EMENEY

Myxomatosis

Myxomatosis was one of my youth's strangest words; its syllables cursed
wild rabbits, small healthy specimens of which I had seen a clutch that year—
wriggling shut-eyed and short-eared in the nest of my granddad's scratchy
  jacket,
brought up from the orchard where he'd found them abandoned one
  morning.
At least that was his story. Had he shot their mother and discovered
them shortly after? I could not have known and would not ask today.

Myxomatosis was on the news and in the boys' worst jokes at school
while Parliament decided whether or not to bring it back for the cull.
Dad told me about 1950s rabbits writhing on roadsides or forest paths
—how he had mercy-killed one in a bluebell wood, and, up close,
had seen the bark-like, leprous eyelids, the pustuled ears. Strange,
these tales during the daytime, which would have terrified me in the dark ...

But people brought up on wartime farms can be like that, turning up with
  armfuls
of orphaned kits one minute, perfect for a granddaughter to feed with an
  eyedropper,
then describing the grisly horrors of myxoma virus to a nine-year-old the
  next.
I blame it on the arcane rules of their youth: that set of maledictions
surrounding survival, extinction and the weighing up of cruelty's necessity.

SARAH HARPUR

Dead Dads Club

People can get a bit squeamish around the subject of dead dads. I can see where they're coming from but there's no need for alarm—dads have been dying since the 1960s.

Misfortune in life is not enjoyable but you learn from it. It makes you stronger, more resilient. No one became a decent person by getting everything they want. Cigarette burns taught me that Granddad needs space.

If you are reading this and your dad is not of the dead persuasion, please relax. I assure you that reading this will not jinx him. Your dad will be fine.

But maybe don't read it *to* him. Or print out a copy, frame it and send it to him. Dads don't like to consider their own deaths and they don't like their children to consider them either. It may impact on the quality of your next birthday present. But at least your dad can still buy you presents! Because he's not dead.

Our dad died in January 1998. Our favourite cousin lost her dad in September that same year. The Dead Dads Club is what happens when you combine four bereaved teenagers and come back two decades later.

Before I get too carried away it's worth pointing out three things:

We're Fine. Our dads died a long time ago—one of those classic things in life that are difficult at the time, funny in hindsight.

Seriously, we're Fine. Dads are like wisdom teeth. Losing them is painful, but you'll only have to go through it once.

We are so Fine that people don't believe we're Fine and they try to psychoanalyse us. 'How can a person be Fine with having a dead dad? Come on, you psychopath, cry!'

Grief is a long and crazy process. You have a short while to navigate this minefield before you are released back into the wild. Take a deep breath. Everything is Fine.

Most of us will be familiar with the five stages of grief: Denial, Bargaining, Anger, Depression and Acceptance. These stages were identified in Elisabeth Kübler-Ross's 1969 book *On Death and Dying*. Perfect summer reading. Tuck it under your arm, spread out your towel, then devour it cover to cover on a white-sand beach while sipping a cocktail garnished with a cheerful novelty umbrella. Breathe deeply and know that death awaits us all. Anyone for tennis?

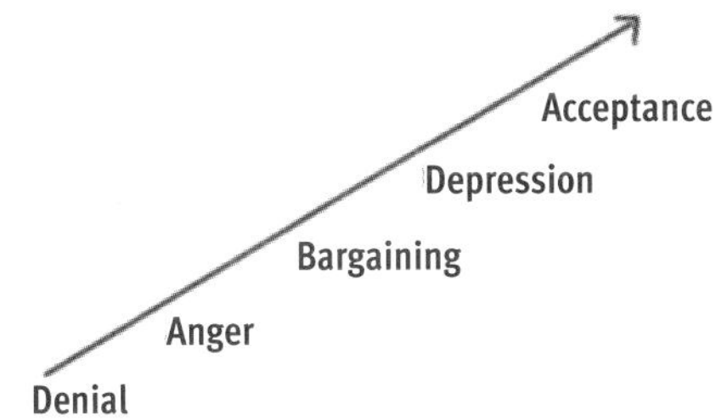

Figure 1. The Five Phases of Grief

The five stages of grief were ground-breaking, but are now seen as problematic. People have latched on to this concept, clung to it like a how-to manual ('Grieving for Dummies'). This has given rise to the concept of grief as a linear process, where we neatly move from one stage to the next until we graduate at the point of 'Acceptance'.

But in reality, grief is messy. The stages do exist, but you might experience all of them at once, or you might skip an entire stage altogether.

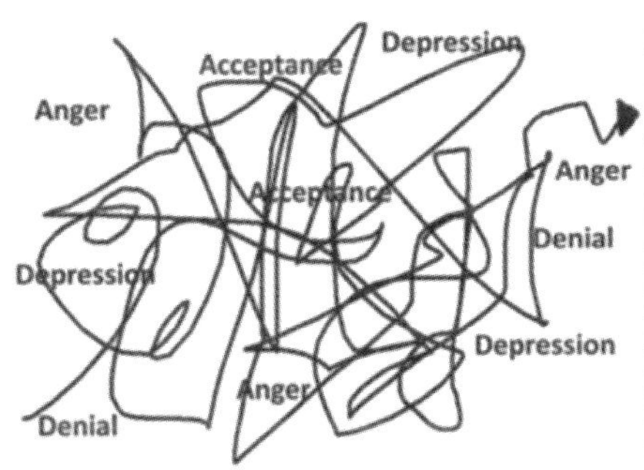

Figure 2. Reality

I have also identified additional stages of grief: KFC, Buying Dogs, Attempts at Humour, and Consulting Psychics.

My sisters and I have spent a long time in the Acceptance phase. I think it's because our dad was always going to die.

Our parents lived in Tokoroa, where I should've been born. Then Dad had a massive car crash and broke his pelvis in sixteen places. He spent a month in Waikato Hospital, so that's where I arrived—first-born, jaundiced, with a notorious appetite. I was born in Hamilton by accident.

It was never confirmed but I think we can safely say that Dad was not sober at the time of his accident. This was 1980s New Zealand, when drink-driving was less a crime, more a way of life.

An example. Mum and Dad were married in Dannevirke. After celebrating for twelve hours, Dad drove them back to their honeymoon suite in Woodville. Weaving along State Highway 2, Dad covered his eye with one hand.

'Mike! What are you doing!'

'It's for your safety,' slurred my father. 'Otherwise there are two roads. God, I love you.'

That man was always going to die.

After Dad's accident his left leg was five centimetres shorter than his right. His left knee could now bend sideways. Everything was a bit bung, like an cheap imitation Barbie Doll.

He had to wear a special shoe with the sole built up. It's been theorised that his look sparked the Spice Girls platform sneaker trend, but this cannot be confirmed.

Dad survived that car crash but it didn't take long for us to realise he wasn't one of those immortal dads. The first heart attack happened when I was five. All I remember is the helicopter. Dad was delirious and asked if they could fly it upside down.

From then on his heart was essentially a faultline. It might rupture in a thousand years or ... NOW! Kids would say, 'My dad could beat your dad in a fight!' We'd agree.

We kids lived in constant fear that we'd be the cause of The Big One. I'm sure he used that fear against us. We'd be minding our own business: doing a jigsaw, reading, watching cartoons—and Dad would stumble into the room clutching his chest. We'd leap up. 'Should we call an ambulance?'

Dad would look at me through scrunched-up eyes. 'Cuppa tea? Extra strong. One sugar.' I hated the day I was deemed old enough to make hot drinks.

Because my dad had a bung leg and a dodgy heart he wasn't allowed to work any more. It wasn't easy for a man like my father to be idle, so he found productive ways to fill his time. Like welding things that didn't need welding. And gambling on the horses.

As a kid I thought it was normal to sit in the car for two hours outside the TAB. This was a time when leaving your kids in the car while you gambled was less a crime, more an obvious childcare solution.

Usually, though, Dad would make bets over the phone and then we'd have to be QUIET as he listened to the race over his transistor radio. We hated that radio. It stood on top of the microwave, propping up unpaid bills, a monument of shhhhhhhh.

Horses raced through our childhood. Interrupted every conversation. Those horses, with their tiny riders and their stupid names. What is so wrong with naming a horse Simon?

Dad had multiple heart operations, but the successes didn't last. In 1998 he needed a new aorta valve. We knew our dad was mortal, but we never expected it would be suicide.*

***Disclaimer**

Now that the 'S' word has been mentioned, it would be irresponsible—nay ILLEGAL—not to include a disclaimer.

Don't commit suicide. It's BAD. Have you thought of taking a lovely walk or joining a yoga class? Some people like to take deep breaths of fresh air. Have you been outside lately? Had a shower?

If you still feel like suiciding, here's a number: 0800 DONTDOIT. Call it! Reach out!

Suicide will make your family sad. They won't blame themselves—until someone asks, 'Do you blame yourself?' which will make them wonder if they should.

They will also be asked, 'Did they leave a note?' We're not in a note-leaving zeitgeist, but if you absolutely insist on committing suicide, it's only polite. This way, your family can make photocopies of the suicide note and a keep a copy in their wallet, just in case the subject comes up. And it will.

Every conversation is six degrees of separation from suicide. Your loved one might go to the supermarket for some Vogel's and a bag of onions and start talking about weather—which is a segue into family, which is a segue into 'What do they do for a living?', which is a segue into the fact they *aren't* living, which is a segue into 'How did they die?', which is a segue into suicide, which is a segue into 'Why did they do it?'—which is the ideal time to present the stranger with their very own copy of your suicide note so they can get back to contemplating which brand of milk is more likely to make them fat.

Don't kill yourself. Suicide is the least socially acceptable way to die. Other socially unacceptable ways of death include climbing into the Sumatran tiger's cage at your local zoo and autoerotic asphyxiation.

If you kill yourself, your loved ones will make inappropriate jokes. They'll find other people who understand and they'll laugh about it. Because grief is like Dannevirke—just because you have to drive through it sometimes, doesn't mean you have to buy a house there.

They'll joke about killing themselves if there is bad WiFi coverage or if they run out of coffee or if they step on a crack. This is NOT good. It devalues suicide, and we cannot have a society that doesn't FREAK OUT if we say the 'S' word. It must always be said gravely. It must always be the worst thing.

Your loved ones must never make peace with your suicide, because if they do, then they are accepting it as an option, which it must NEVER be.

We must rage and fight—celebrities must punch each other in the face to raise awareness—but we cannot joke or accept suicide because we need to maintain a CONSTANT STATE OF OUTRAGE if we are ever to fix this problem.

One day you'll be okay. You'll be glad you didn't kill yourself because there's a lot of great TV you haven't watched and a lot of weird novelty chocolate flavours that Whittaker's haven't yet released.

Patience is key. You'll die eventually, I promise.

It was our uncle who told us about Dad. As soon as I saw our uncle's face I knew it was bad news. It's like those times you enter a public toilet cubicle and the toilet lid is down. You approach cautiously. You hold your breath and hope for the best. But deep inside you know it's shit.

It's strange when your life changes forever in an instant, but the world carries on as normal. The radio was on and as we were trying to process the sudden and permanent loss of our father; live on air, one of the presenters was getting his butt waxed. He yelled, 'Oh god! You bastard! It hurts!' That was the first time a radio jock said something I could relate to.

So our dad was dead and we were plunged into the role of bereaved teens. Apparently we didn't grieve appropriately. Kids at school heard about our dad's death and thought it was a rumour. How could it be true? Those girls are wearing colour and I've never seen them cry. Is that normal?

My youngest sister was ten. Her school books brimmed with poems devoted to Dad. They contained fragments of plagiarised lyrics from our parents' Time Life CD library, *The Emotions Collection*. This collection of twelve CDs was split in two when Mum and Dad separated, and reunited after he died.

Thanks to *The Emotions Collection*, my sister's poems for Dad spoke of a romantic love. She wanted to see 'deep into his blue eyes' and was 'hungry for his touch'. Her teacher insisted these poems were a healthy outlet. My other sister and I were horrified. Somehow those poems were lost. Such a pity.

When someone dies, you have to learn to speak in code, because no one will ever speak honestly about them again. All their flaws will be remembered as endearing character quirks:

Your dad ...

- was such a character! (borderline criminal)
- was a real ladies' man! (a bit creepy)
- liked a drink! (alcoholic)
- was strong willed! (a nightmare)
- never really saw eye to eye (hated that guy).

No one joins the Dead Dads Club by choice, but there are pros as well as cons. On the one hand, it's a devastating loss. On the other, I got two weeks off school. The pros and cons continue:

- PRO: I don't have to be quiet during the rugby

- CON: My parents will never grow old together
- PRO: I'll never walk in on them having sex.

Burying a parent is tough. But it's better than the other way around. It's them or you.

The undisputed major benefit of having a dead dad is holding the sympathy card. Unfortunately, sympathy has an expiry date. It's highest before you're 47.5 years of age. Please see Figure 3, which charts the rise and decline in sympathy that one might receive upon admission into the Dead Dads Club:

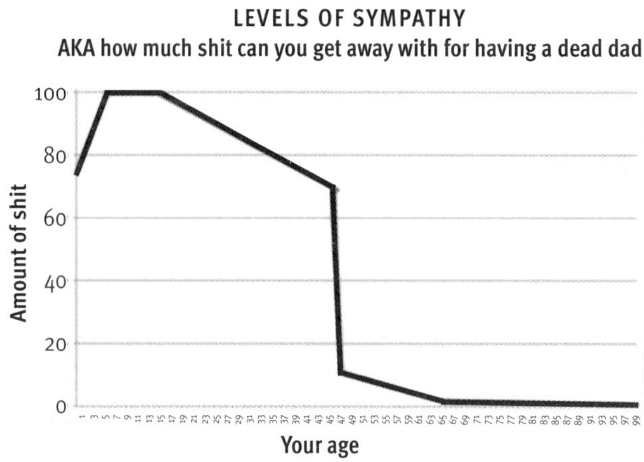

Figure 3. Rise and Decline of Sympathy

This graph illustrates how much you can get away with, according to how old you are when your dad dies. As you can see, babies get a decent amount of sympathy, but not at maximum levels. This is because of their lack of emotional investment in other humans. Babies are cold.

Sympathy peaks at age four, and stays high until age eighteen, when you reach adulthood. Then it starts to decline. However, you can still enjoy sympathy at about 80 percent capacity over the next two decades.

But something happens when you turn 47.5. There is a drastic decline in sympathy because at age 47.5 you hit Peak Dead Dad. This is the age when, statistically speaking, you are more likely to have a dead dad than not.

Peak Dead Dad is calculated by taking average male life expectancy, which is 79.5. From this figure, we subtract the average age of fathers of new babies, which is 32. We are left with the age of 47.5 = Peak Dead Dad.

From this point onwards, if your dad dies, you'll get your three days' bereavement leave and society will expect you to be Fine.

Grief is a minefield. People say the wrong thing all the time. No one means to. They see their loved ones in pain and they want to fix it. And they want it fixed immediately, so they'll say anything to try and make it better:

'Your dad's an angel now.'

Yes, Aunty Barbara. My 47-year-old dad from Tokoroa is an angel. He's up in heaven, wearing a frilly white dress:

'I'm not gay! I'm an angel. I love rugby. The way those strong athletic men relentlessly pound each other into the ground ... I'm not gay. I'm an angel ...'

Dad's angel dress has lasagne stains all over it, and he's not even embarrassed because in New Zealand in the nineties lasagne was very fancy. 'See that stain? That's lasagne. Have you tried it? It's Italian.'

My angel father spends his days up in heaven rubbing his wings together at speed, trying to create enough friction to light the sixteen Pall Mall menthols he's got wedged between the digits on his hands and feet. He smokes his cigarettes one by one, holding them between the ill-fitting false teeth he got when he was nineteen years old because he went to a dentist who told him he needed ONE tooth pulled out, and Dad said, 'Why don't you pull them all out?'

And the dentist said, 'Okay, I will.'

And Dad said, 'Do it then.'

And the dentist said, 'I bloody will.'

And Dad said, 'Do it with my blessing.'

And the dentist said, 'I don't need your blessing, I need you to sign this form.'

And Dad said, 'I don't have a pen.'

And the dentist said, 'Here's a pen!'

And Dad said, 'Good.'

---

1 When we look at life expectancy, it is important to let you know this is not a guarantee, according to a lengthy disclaimer on Statistics New Zealand's website. It seems that life expectancy is like avocados—not covered under the Consumer Guarantees Act.

And the dentist said 'Do you want anaesthetic?'

And Dad said, 'I'm not gay.'

So thank you, Aunty Barbara. Yes, my dad is an angel. What a comforting thought.

The most helpful words of comfort were bestowed upon Cousin Hayleigh at her father's funeral. We stood around Uncle Terry's grave and, as the coffin was lowered into the ground, Hayleigh began to cry—as you might at your father's funeral.

Kevin, a family friend, leaned in, held Hayleigh's shoulder and whispered, 'I used to cry because I didn't have shoes, and then I met a man who didn't have feet.'

Beautiful words.

First of all, Kevin. Crying because you don't have shoes? Ridiculous. This is New Zealand. We don't wear shoes. We call them foot oppressors. The soles of my feet are so thick I can dance on thumbtacks.

Secondly, Kevin. What if you're a man without feet, and you have a cry—as you might when you have no feet—and then you meet a man without any legs?

And then, Kevin, what if you're a man without any legs, and you have a cry—as you might when you can't do Zumba—and then you meet a man who's just a bellybutton? That's right, he's a semi-conscious piece of sinew, resting on a velvet pillow.

Kevin was making a valid point: There is always someone worse off than you, so stop crying, because it makes Kevin uncomfortable.

I say cry. It's good for you; it stops your eyeballs from drying out. Just don't cry in front of a man who is only a bellybutton.

Many club members get comfort from the concept of Heaven. I have no desire to debate its existence, but to me, Heaven sounds like hell.

You've must believe whatever brings you comfort. I'm not comforted by the concept of Heaven but I do believe that my dad is still with us. He's still in our lives if we think about him, talk about him, laugh about him. My relationship with Dad is exactly like Patrick Swayze and Demi Moore's in *Ghost*. With less pottery.

In my mind, Dad spends his days protecting us from bad guys. He's in the scattering of autumn leaves, rolling around the ditch, batting our ankles. He's an invisible force-field, he karate chops would-be attackers. He throws sand in their eyes and spits rain in their face. On a good day, he's in the try-scoring roar at Eden Park. On a bad day, he slaps the ref.

We still have a dad. He just happens to be dead.

Ultimately the Dead Dads Club is about solidarity. It's about connecting with others who won't judge you for rolling about in the awkwardness of grief like a pig in mud.

I made my dad a Facebook profile so he could thank my sister for posting how she missed him. Some of the family loved his social media presence. Other's weren't fans of the concept. I would like to make it clear that I realise that making a Facebook profile as your dead father might not be the most mentally stable thing you could do. But I have to say my heart skipped a beat when he friend-requested me. It may be inappropriate, but how can there be an appropriate way to grieve? There's nothing appropriate about losing your dad.

Grief is different for everyone. But there will come a day when you're Fine.

I can't tell you when that will be. You might be Fine now. It might take months, years or even decades.

Being Fine might be a gradual realisation, or one day it might slap you around the side of the face like a dildo at a press conference. But when you realise you're Fine, that can be as scary and confronting as not being Fine. We're so conditioned to know the appropriate responses to loss. But what about the other ones?

Elisabeth Kübler-Ross apparently felt terrible about the way her five stages of grief were misinterpreted. In the last days of her life she said, 'I am more than these five stages. And so are you.'

I'd like to finish by suggesting one more stage: 'Making up for regrets.' I never spoke at Dad's funeral. And if you were to psychoanalyse me, it would seem I've spent the last twenty years making up for it. So, here's a belated eulogy:

My dad was a Bit of a Character. We didn't always see eye to eye. But I always knew that he loved me ferociously. I long for his touch.

We're Fine. Honestly.

PATRICIA GRACE

Green Dress

These words, which are barred behind my clamped-down teeth—teeth that have a pair of sealed-off lips to the fore of them—are not incarcerated there because of what I wore to my wedding. The colour green has nothing to do with any of what's happening right here, now, despite what my mother may think.

Soon, say in less than an hour, these lips will part, the teeth will unclench and words will be let out. In the meantime they stay locked in there, live as bees. My mother won't like them.

There'll be a ladder. The arrival of a ladder and, I hope, the arrival of my mother, is what the words are being held until. If Mum's been told what's happened by the one who rang her to get my phone number, then she'll come for sure. Let her come. Let her hear what will emanate from me, here on my hands and knees, at the edge of the hole, staring down. I hope she makes it. She's got to hear.

Maybe a policeman will turn up.

There's a bereaved family somewhere, preparing to make its way here, not knowing the hole made ready for the burial of their loved one is occupied. But it's okay. They're not due for a couple of hours, so they need never know about you down there, eyes shut, pretending to be dead, stretched out long and skinny and kinked at either end, like a white bean, wearing only your fernleaf boxers. I bought you those. The whole drama'll be over by the time that grieving whānau gets here.

And jandals. Undies and jandals. Why undies and jandals? Clothes and boots left in a pile on the fake grass covering the yellow mound. Viz vest on top, and your phone.

I shot up here after the phone call from Tali who had done his best to persuade you out of there. 'He's not dead,' he said over the phone.

'Course not,' I said. Just mad, I thought.

I've known Tali since we were at school together. He rang Mum who gave him my work number. Don't know what he told her.

When I arrived, Tali showed me to this site here and said he was going to get a ladder, but first had to get a key to a shed so he could get the ladder. He'd be back in half an hour. Said he'd rung the boss. Said the boss was out of town but he'd got hold of the cops.

'It's not going to happen, Marlie,' Mum said when I told her you and I were getting married. That was five years ago. We had this row, Mum and me. Reminded her I was twenty-five and could make up my own mind. Don't usually stand up to Mum, but this time ... well, she never approved of anyone I brought home anyway.

'Not good enough,' she said.

'You always say that ...'

'Lame dogs, wet ducks, losers.' Nutting off, she was.

'Look who's talking,' I said.

'My only daughter, only child born to me, what would your father think, what'll Jerry say?' Nutting off, nutting off.

'Dad's dead,' I said, 'and it doesn't matter what Jerry says. It's me, Mum.' I knocked my stiff middle finger into my chest, tap tap, like finding hollow spaces in a wall, making the same sound. 'Me. What I think, what I say. For once.'

'What about Jerry?'

'Wet ducks doesn't make sense,' I said.

'Whatever whatever.'

'And anyway what about "aroha ki te tangata"— you're always spouting on about that. "Ahakoa ko wai ..."'

'It means compassion towards all people, no matter who, no matter where from. Kindness,' Mum said. 'That's what it's about. Doesn't mean you got to marry them.'

I didn't want to listen to any more of that so started listing the lame ducks, wet puppies etc—all the brothers and sisters she and Dad had brought home over the years, starting with Jerry who Dad found in a bus stop sleeping under a strip of blue tarp. Sixteen years old. Brought him home, warmed him up in the shower, fed him, put him in bed. He became our big brother.

'He took you everywhere,' Mum said. 'Jerry. You did everything together, you and him. Kids on skateboards going to the dairy, him with a pushchair. He didn't care. Dancing along. Or you on his back, horsing around, bouncing on tramps.'

Diverted from the topic of my marriage for the moment we talked about Jerry and Tutty. Two days after Tutty's arrival she stole Mum's car. Me and Jerry found it parked by the bridge, Tutty parked under it—the bridge—sniffing glue with teens. We dragged her home. She was supposed to be our sister. She is our sister. We made her be it.

And Dolene. Newborn. Named her myself. 'Dolene,' I said when Mum brought her home from work at CYFS, now renamed Oranga Tamariki. They're the ones who stayed—Jerry, Tutty, Dolene. Then Jerry went into the army, followed by Tutty ten years later. Dolene's still at home with Mum, the two of them rattling around in that big house, everyone else gone. Then there were all the in-betweens who stayed six months, a year, two years, two weeks, until a situation changed and they moved on. They come back, in and out, Christmas, write us cards, ring up. Get home from work: 'A card from your sister', 'The twins rang up,' all that stuff.

Mum and I are mates, we're good mates. She's, you know, good. Good. To everyone, whoever. We looked after them. Her, Dad, me. Cuddled them, bathed them, played in the park. Jerry too but he had a job washing dishes, then he got accepted. Big brother soldier. Their beds. Their teeth. Cute. All ready for school. Homework. I liked the homework. Whoever whoever, didn't matter, sniffing glue, orphaned, abandoned, runaway, whoever, so what's the problem now?

'Got a job, he don't smoke, hardly drinks, got a place to live, wouldn't hurt a flea. Like you always said, Mum, "No losers, users or abusers", so, what's the problem now?'

'He's got mad eyes,' she said.

I walked out. Mum's never allowed us to do that. You got a problem, you gotta be there to be part of the solution. 'Come back here,' she called, but it took me five circuits of the park before I could do that.

When I got back, 'He loves me, Mum, really loves me. Really. And we *are* getting married.'

'You're not short on love, Daughter,' she said. 'There's plenty who love you. Your father idolised you, your big brother the same. The whole world to us, you. We don't want to see ...'

'You don't know him, Mum.'

'And why's that? Brings you home, won't stop for a feed, five minutes and he's out the door. Next thing I go out, see him sitting out there in his car, watching.'

'You're against him because he's a Pākehā,' I said. Stupid thing to say.

'Oh, a Pākehā, just like your father,' she said, 'who I loved 'til the day he died and ever after. Like Dolene and two of the other kids who became our family. What a load of crap.' And then *she* walked out.

'We better talk about this wedding?' she said when she came back some minutes later with red eyes and a washed, damp face.

'Thanks, Mum,' I said. 'It's just he's shy, doesn't like a lot of people.'

'Better get over himself if he's coming here to live.'

I didn't want to tell her, but had to, that you had your own place and we were going to live there.

'Renting?' she asked.

'For now,' I said.

'Why would you want to do that when we got this big house, all these bedrooms and bathrooms? Tell him.'

But I didn't. So it was us married and you and me in a house, you following me about in it, watching, going through my clothes and bags.

Not dead but too far down to detect breathing. Not even the tremor of an eyelid. Stretched out like that other time, pathetic, on the kitchen floor, after I'd been to see Mum on her birthday.

'She never comes to see you, so why?' you said. 'They never come to see you. And who's all going to be there?'

'Come with me,' I said. 'Jerry's home.'

'How would you know that?

'Mum rang me at work.'

'That's what you do all day at work, gab on the phone to your mum? What sort of a job is that?' On and on. 'He's not your real brother. What's going on?' You were waiting for me to give in, as I usually did, but I hadn't been home for months and had made up my mind. 'Come with me.' Relieved when you refused.

Later that evening, came home to a house in darkness, opened the door, switched on the light. Out on the floor. Like a TV murder scene, or a kids' board game—Mad Martin, in the Kitchen, with a Knife. Except there was no knife, no blood. I took you in my arms. We held each other. I put the heater on. You said you were sorry. You said you'd missed me, said you'd come with me next time.

Yeah, right.

Following, following. Room to room.

Mum got her way about the wedding. 'Just you and me, Babe,' you said, but Mum wouldn't have any of that. I managed to talk you round. We did it all. Whole family: grannies, aunties, uncles, cousins. Church, flowers, bridesmaids, groomsmen, three-tier cake, big reception at the boating club. Cooking? We did it all ourselves.

But I couldn't talk you out of the green dress you thought I should wear. You'd had no say in anything else, you kept reminding me, and wanted to choose the fabric that went best with my eyes. I wondered about that, the eyes, expecting we'd be looking through white crêpe, chiffon, georgette, jacquard, satin, velour, tulle. You took to plum blossom green brocade and nothing would change your mind. Also, I thought it very pretty and could see myself in it.

'Not green,' Mum said. 'No way.'

'It matches my eyes.'

'Your eyes are brown,' she pointed out, then started in on funerals.

'Bad luck, is what I'm saying. What do you see when someone dies? You see green. Verandah decorated with kawakawa leaves, women with greenery in their hair swishing their green branches.'

That all seemed like a big exaggeration to me, unless she was thinking of the tangihanga of Te Arikinui Dame Te Atairangikaahu. But I felt sorry for Mum. I know she was only saying what others might think, so I shouldn't've said what I did.

'Get over yourself, Mum. You don't even half believe what you're saying.'

'You're wrong there,' she said. 'I do half believe it.'

But I know it was the marriage she was against, not the colour of the dress. Aunty Julie made it up for me. High collar, little sleeves, pencil skirt. Chinesey. Plenty of nice comments about it on the wedding day.

Stones cutting into my knees. That's Tali's van coming with the ladder, and yep, police car down there pulling in to the carpark.

Behind those shut-down lids are bright blue ovals. Pretty. All over me, every minute. Or. Going through my phone, my photos. Delete, delete. While I waited for life to be better.

There's this thing about hope. It's supposed to be what you hold in your heart. There's hope and there's kindness. Kindness is what I'm good at: warm bed, cuddles, listening, praise and compliments.

'Kindness, love and cross your fingers,' Mum says, 'and it don't matter who.'

Well, 'cross your fingers' means you give out kindness then you hope for the best. But it's 'hope' that leads you on, is my conclusion now. One day, one day, one day, cross fingers, it'll be all right. Sorry, Babe. Flowers. Sorry, sorry. Promise, promise. Is hope such a good thing to keep in your heart? Forever and ever?

Nah. It stymies you, holds you down. You hope, you hope, you hope, and you weaken, you fade, you stay home, you don't visit, you start to believe words: They don't care about you. Why should you care? They never ring you. Why ring them? Why write to him? He's never written to you? He's not real family. I'm it. Me. Not him. Nag, nag. What for? Who? Why, why, why? Why should? Why shouldn't? Stunts. Sorry, sorry. Promise, promise. Stunts.

So, who am I now?

My photo of Dolene—who I named, who has crafty eyes and fairy hair. I made her dresses. I bought her shoes. She bit my finger with her tooth. She walked to me—torn in half.

A letter arrived from my brother Jerry, arrived at work. He was married and had two kids I'd never seen. He had special leave. We didn't know at the time that he had an overseas posting. He and his family were coming home for Labour Weekend. He'd contacted all our brothers and sisters and there was going to be a big reunion on the Saturday and Sunday. Full house, he said.

You came home, read the letter and threw it in the recycling but I couldn't not go. Couldn't not.

'I'm going,' I said.

'So snaps his fingers and you come running? No way.'

'I'm going. I'm getting new clothes.'

You sat across the doorway with your face hanging.

Stepped over you and went to bed.

The next morning you made coffee and toast and said you were coming to the party too. You were coming shopping with me for my outfit. I didn't want you to come, either shopping or to the party, but okay.

I bought a pant suit, a new top, strappy sandals and some makeup. You didn't like any of it. I'd had nothing new since the green dress.

An hour after we arrived you wanted to go home. 'We got to get back,' you said. 'Landlord's coming for an inspection.' You'd used that excuse before. This time it happened to be true but I'd arranged for her to visit in our absence. She didn't mind. Our place was always up to scratch.

'You go if you want, I'm staying,' I said. He couldn't gripe too much with the family around. I walked out into the kitchen and began cutting long sausage rolls into bite-sized bits ready for baking.

Next minute, there you were hovering in the doorway.

'We gotta go,' you said.

'She's not going anywhere,' Mum said, brushing past him with a load of plates. 'She's staying put, right here.'

You said nothing, went into a sulk, stood around, wouldn't eat a thing. Then you left. Thank god.

We cleaned up, put on music and sang and danced. Danced with Jerry, Leonie, their kids, all the brothers and sisters. Danced Dolene round and round. Jerry said, 'Come for a holiday, Sis. Get away for a bit. Or forever?'

Later we set up a table of leftovers for the evening meal. Others did that while I bathed Dolene. Bony, creamy, scabby girl. Sapphire eyes. Flaky creases. Glassy hair, sparse, delicate like daddy-long-legs legs. Same colour.

And I thought of you at home lying on the floor, in the bath with scratched wrists, hanging purple in the shower, smashed mirror, crimson feet full of glass.

Woke up in bed with faces above.

'Where's Dolene?'

'In bed asleep. You gotta ... we gotta ...'

'I think I fainted.'

'Fainting don't last an hour, two hours.'

Big lumps of crying.

You turned up next morning: sorry, sorry, sorry.

'I'm going to Linton for a holiday,' I said.

'No.' 'Can't.' 'What about work?' 'Can't.' 'What about ... ?'

'You'll survive,' Leonie said on her way out to the van with gear. Leonie should mind her own business, I thought. Mum was staring me down, the whole gang packing gear, packing their cars, their kids, talking, laughing. Going.

Into the van, crying in lumps. Jerry with his foot down, shooting away in case I changed my mind.

I spent two weeks off work on sick leave. At the end of that time I rang and told you I'd be returning to work but living with Mum and Dolene.

Crying. Going home to Mum. Who was I then?

Who am I now?

Tali, with Mum hurrying up behind on fat legs. Tali stops, takes her arm. They come, slow. He lets go her arm and eases the ladder down.

Cops standing by.

Mum flops down beside me, red. My lips part and teeth unclench. I pull in a breath. She's got to hear this.

But it's Mum who speaks. Her voice, her words saying what I was going to say, only in a different way.

'Get up outta there, you.'

Eyelids lift. Blue orbs.

'Taking you home with us and no nonsense.'

There's movement.

'Get a move on before I change my mind.'

Coming up, mud-spattered. Sorry, sorry.

'Sorry don't wash with me. Shut up about sorry. Put your clothes on. Get home, get in the shower. Any more crap from you and you're out the door, hear me?'

Ladder coming up. Cops leaving. Pulling on clothes while looking sideways. Bereaved family assembling down in the carpark.

Fingers crossed, heart bounding.

JO-ELLA SARICH

The Jasmine (We need to talk about suicide)

That summer the jasmine
found the nooks in the weatherboard, found
me in the bath, the sweet intruder. Our parents
once loved in monochrome, insouciant moons
half-turned towards the sun. In the mirror
I can barely distinguish the parts of myself any more. When I was young
I knew how to love
like a tractor facing up the might of a hill.
Now
I turn
my arms into right angles to see if they will carry my weight, but I only see
your sinew in my brow line. My lack of focus. Look, the birds
are squirrelling tiny things under the eaves. Who are
you now, the present wiping away
the trees that once carpeted the yard?
Someone called it tūrangawaewae. So I pretend
I speak Dutch; arch my tongue back
to invoke my uvular. Invoke my mother
who loved
with the vexation of the bobbin under a Tom Thumb light.
when I was young I used to love
like the twisted damson tree that never failed
to fill our buckets. The dam that drank the hills. The still of the land before it
was answered by the rain. We need to talk
about something other than
            The monochrome
            The working parts
            About the words 'any more'
            The day the policeman
came he seemed irked by our pop-out storybook world. When I was young I tore
the jasmine out by its roots, convinced it was spying on me.

TALIA MARSHALL

Being Active

My cousin goes to more than one Countdown
To spend her benefit on water and apples
For Ihumātao, she picks me up from Manukau
And tells me she was standing with a mate
And her mate said what are those Pākehā doing here?
As they watched them build a barricade out of supermarket trolleys
My cousin laughs and tells her to leave them be
So they can get arrested first

She says I should come out to Ihumātao
But I offer to babysit even though the kids want to go too
She says, 'Don't you write about that kind of thing cuz?
It would be good for you to see it', but I'm still
Just trying to be it plus I might see someone I know

I say we could go home and do it there
Because even the bones are busy
She says it's a good thing my father kept me away from the family
Because no one is allowed to call themselves useless
And I take her cue and wash the dishes

I ask her who Aunty Coggy was, who was Aunty Bang?
She says Aunty Coggy lived in the house by the first bend
In the river after the tracks, oh I know that house
The one that's grey, uneasy and tagged to bits

It would be good to hear it laughing again let's go

From her verandah with the Tino flag she surveys the harbour

And says Google Maps doesn't show you the best waka route to Ihumātao

Once I've gone she writes that the fruit sponge
rising in the oven turned out beautiful
And later she let off fireworks with the kids hoping they could see them in Ihumātao.

I want them for us too, these tūpuna waving sparklers in the sky
And the great turning she walked into the water for last October, the gears shifting down as my father died and the moon turned into a lotus for her

A pearl

I send her the thumb emoji because I could do more but she is, she is.

JOHN ALLISON

The Tragedy of Learning

(for Martha, aged 3 years)

her language is becoming ours
it is a gain it is a loss
words are magic
but it is in the nature of spells
that they are less effective with use
still, I try once more

do you want to play your *voison*?
I say it in the French way
having learned it from her: vwa.zõ
she looks at me
violin, she says, violin
and turns away

ESSA MAY RANAPIRI

echidna goes to see the drone perform in front of a live audience

after Harry Josephine Giles' Drone

echidna sits in the crowd while the drone hums her song in the air
watches as she just hangs there
in glitter shine w/ two layers of lipstick
suspended on blades that spin and spin and spin
it is a drone making a *droooone*
noise   the notes are waterfalling to spit against the ground

the drone shares a story in the splash
about her cat
about being a woman with a dick that hangs limp between her drone legs
   (nervous at a party   talking to some militarised version
            of argus panoptes
alllllll of the eyes are watching)
about her job experience
about the violence inherent
or inherited in the
experience of   of   of   of
there are bees in the slideshow behind her
worker bees in a colony
the drone that is a pun   or a punishing tonic   to   the rhetoric of sale of
selling of buying of   of of of of

echidna can't help but cry as the drone places her own head in the filing
   cabinet
as the drone prays for a quiet death at home

not a falling apart inside any number of her targets

echidna wonders if the pot-plant is in there too? the filing cabinet
she can't quite remember
that fragile lick of nature   of something we made of something they made us
do

buying out selling out out out out out   there

echidna is inside the panopticon   trying to reach out and save the drone
from her preprogrammed cycle   the whirr that won't stop

*

the pātere that stretches between
her the drone and
her the mother of monsters
is nothing like the orders either are used to
the doctrine of divide and subtract
of work yourself to the bone
the carbon fibre frame trembling
in wire network fizz

where they both hold on to either end of the string
the pūrerehua spins and disrupts the air
as they step into a different world
moving hands towards each other and back
coil and uncoil
flinging air in a way
that catches the tragedy of the situation
in the husk of the laughter that bumps against the stage lights

MARK EDGECOMBE

Lun

I don't remember his arriving.
It was as if he'd always been here.

He was the boy from Kampuchea,
Prince of Standard Four,

Cambodian Fonz, his
bomber jacket zipper

at half-mast. That much
was imitable, if not his knack

for finding the under-half
of the goalpost's H,

his touch defter, demeanour
humbler than any of his peers',

his pivot on scoring immediate—
no urge to pump fist or

beat breast, only the barest
of smiles sideways, cast

at us in Standard Two,
as if letting us in on a joke.

When our class photo was taken,
the photographer made

me zip my jacket
all the way up to the neck.

RUSHI VYAS

Portrait of Bapu's Hand as Brueghel's *Icarus* with Rilke and a Swami in It

Now he is opening the box, the boy
opening, the father above looking on,
hair combed and flowing like blackened fronds

of a willow, arching above the scalp as the boy hides behind the lid
as if it is a simile, as if he does not wish to know
what is cupped in the box, which the boy pretends

might carry more than the letters of a fading booklet
with an ochre-robed brahmin man on the cover
and its title, *Thoughts of Power*.

                                        The father's hand swings up
and lands gently on the boy's hair, strokes
side to side the black like a pond ebbs

after catching a body that flew too close
to the sun. The father is a pink sky
after monsoons, unknowable. The father,

in affection, holds shoulders
like an undetermined tense, like a boy
too young for fluency in the body

language of one brow here another
below the bridge, where snow stifles
the certain world.

The boy closes
the box. He looks to the father through
eyes white with the season of unknowing

trying to remember what he will
pretend to forget: an open palm
caressing his hair like the shruti note of rain

blown diagonal by northwest wind, hammering
the corner of a roof and streaming down
to collect, like a child, wherever will let it return.

MICHAEL GIACON

To Everything, a Season

Through glass, inside faces out.
Cloud across blue, paintings against white
sunshine on unpolished floor, the artist spotlit,
she talks of brush movement as showers stroke iron.
Outside also sits here, last week, framed by farewells
through final hours, then the sudden release to peace.

The Q&A confirms the arrangement of the room. Coiled
colours flank an arched window, anointed sculptures lean
to bare trees reaching. She's young, sincere, vibrant
acrylic full of grace. I knead a handkerchief saved
from my father's desk but can't stem
what's missing without, within.

EMER LYONS

nothing repaired, nothing gained

the aftermath of dinner sat in the fridge for a week / broccoli burnt with cheese to pots forever blackened / there is so much these days i can't be bothered with / and so many people same / the only thing i want to do is go into a future i once didn't believe in / my face won't heal as if a sign i am broken / if there is a footstool at the tip shop / will you get it for me? / sadness starts to leak out of me / how much pressure feels good? / i am better than ever at the alphabet / i don't know why i have that letter in my bag after the way she told everyone my laughter was malice / i am getting better at recognising feelings / not having learnt that at school / so many useless things taught / but not how to cope / i was the class clown / warned of self-destruction / i never quietened besides / found someone who gains words from mine / i ask about lemons (x5) and whether that thing the character did / the interrupting like a comma / was something i did / learning mah-jong / and other wholesome things with palettes are how we spend our time / cleaning out the bath so we can soak in moonshine / experimenting happiness / i grow sideways / back forth beyond the here and now / they made efforts to tame us / you can tell me your disappointments / and they won't solidify / they will water in the sun / and i will swim in them / together at opposite ends / we found this / challenging in its pure kind of disaster / i'll fold it to lint in my pockets / take it out with surprise

VINCENT O'SULLIVAN

Splinters

One of the good things about growing old. Her sister Deb had been throwing such phrases about for the past ten years, since before she turned sixty. A flighty, trivial person since she first declared a teenager must be rebellious, and now thought a woman of a certain age—another favoured phrase—would naturally offer wise and interesting remarks. Deb was rich and had problems with her weight, but was kindly, and in several book clubs, and at least voted differently from her husband. Which did not mean for a moment she was not hard to take, almost impossible to like.

Emily realised she was taking a leaf from her sister's book as she looked past the young boy with the pale inquiring face who sat opposite her, to the back yard's tangle of unmown lawn, the shrubs gone wild, the snaggled macrocarpa rising behind it all. 'One of the bad things about getting old,' she heard herself saying, 'is that what used to be quite a pretty garden can get away on you.' She smiled at the pointlessness of saying this to her grandson, who was here to play draughts, which he was obsessed with, while waiting for his mother to pick him up after her appointment. Appointments were frequent but important. They kept caviar on the table, as his father Barry said, meaning it to be a joke, although Donald had no idea why that was funny. He knew though that 'appointments' meant his mother drove people to look at houses, and turned on taps and switches for them so they would know the house worked, and often there was a 'special occasion' when she sold one.

'It's your move, Emily,' the boy reminded her. It was special, he knew that, when he called his grandmother by her real name. Another sort of game between them. It showed what good mates they were. His mother said he shouldn't so he was careful it was only like now, with just the two of them together. His arms, in their grey school jersey with a monogram a bit like the crocodile on the shirt his father wore when he played golf, leaned to either side of the checkered board.

Chit of a thing, Emily thought. Made her think of a bird. As he pressed against her when Meg came to collect him and he said goodbye and thank you for having me, Gran, he might as well have been a bundle of twigs. Which of course was nonsense. He was dead keen on soccer, and whatever else it was he played. He liked to tell her but she wasn't always sure of what he said. 'Nifty', though. He told her that was one of the words the coach used about him. And solid. His defence was solid.

'Yes,' he said, 'there are some things you can't help being good at.'

The boy watched the board without looking up at her. He reached out to put his fingers on one of the pieces, then took them away. 'I've decided to think about it more carefully.' Then he asked her, 'How do you mean, "get away on you"?', bringing them back to that.

'It means it just grows all the time and next thing it's a mess.'

'We've got a man comes in and cuts our lawns. The hedges and things. This big mower. And the clipper works by itself. He holds it and it just goes along the hedge.'

Emily made out her next move was harder to decide on than it was.

'Just get Dave to do it,' Donald said about the garden. 'I can ask him.'

'The trouble is,' his grandmother said, 'I've come to like it like that. The birds love it that way too. Things can be too tidy.'

'And cats, I bet,' Donald said. 'They'd love it like that. Poof!' He made a quick dart with his hand, dabbed at her sleeve, and drew his hand back. Quick as that. Emily taken by surprise, wasn't she just!

'Didn't see that coming, did you?' he said. Very solemn as he said it. Just showed you how quick a cat could be! A touch of amusement there too, Emily thought, when he saw her reaction.

God knows how they'd managed to make something like this between them, Barry her son-in-law, tall and pleased with himself, and Meg with her name on the side of the Lexus she drove and 'No 1 Sales' there beside it, which she pointed out to her mother, as though she couldn't read. 'When you consider the competition with the way the market is. Phew!' She moved her head when she said that, as though following a bullet.

Not a thing you'd say to a soul, but even your own daughter could bore you. Meg and Barry together. 'A power couple'—wasn't that a phrase she had read somewhere? Business breakfasts. Festival concerts. 'I didn't know you liked modern dance, either of you,' Emily had said a month or so back, and Meg told her, 'The important thing with our sort of lifestyle, the calls made on us, is to keep Donald's feet on the ground.'

'As opposed to where?' Emily had asked.

'Mother!' Meg's mock frown of reprimand. 'Why do you think we just love it that he comes here every Friday after school? Eh?' She hugged her mother as she told her, 'Values. Do you think we want to end up with a spoiled brat? We see them all the time. I don't think you realise, Mum, how much we rely on you.'

His grandmother would say, when she presented the boy with the plate of freshly baked melting moments he loved, and the glass of Sprite, a drink that his mother said should be banned, for heaven's sake—didn't Emily appreciate the dental havoc sugar caused?—'Time for our values, Donald.' The boy smiling without answering, aware in some obscure way this was teasing his parents. Both of them.

Emily supposed the boy was clever. He mostly won their games not because she allowed him to, but through his knack of seeing chances on the board more quickly than she did. At other times, when he was bored with reading or playing in the mess of the garden, he sat up at the piano that no one had touched since Meg left home. He played a few simple things quite nicely. Played with feeling even, if she could say that without making the kind of claims that grandparents so easily fell to making. It wouldn't matter in any case if he didn't shine. As Meg had done. As the boy's father still liked to do. She guessed the boy liked spending time with her without having to live up to anything. There were afternoons when she wondered if his occasional listlessness had to do with his already understanding what his parents expected of him. His just sitting there some days in the big armchair, looking out to the grey light beneath the roof-high hedge, the torpor of waiting being rather nice in fact. Not that Emily could really know about what a boy that age might think. They liked each other, that was what mattered. Liked to be in the house with just the two of them.

'You look the way an owl looks when it's watching for mice,' Emily told him, 'when you watch the board like that.'

Donald flapped one hand loosely at her. 'Perhaps I am,' he said. Neither needing to smile because it was just them. They both liked it when they shared a joke and neither had to laugh.

Then, 'That's your mother now,' Emily said. The sound of tyres on the gravel in the drive.

She had to admit Barry was right about that, when he said a year back that when you lived alone a gravel drive could be as good as an alarm. The next week the truck and the workmen were there and there it was, spread and crunchy when you walked on it, in time for Mother's Day.

The boy began to collect the pieces and arrange them in their box.

'You won't have time to beat me again,' she said.

'You never know, Emily. You might have won—if we'd finished.'

'Probably right,' she said. 'I was feeling lucky.'

Donald looked at her. 'I was humouring you,' he said. 'Mum said I'm good at that.'

'I don't think you do,' Emily told him. The slightest bit hurt.

'I told her we don't have to try about anything.' The boy chattering on, liking it that he could tell his grandmother something he knew his mother hadn't meant him to.

Meg was calling from the kitchen. 'Can you get a move on, Donny, you know Dad likes us being on time.'

'I know, I know,' the boy said quietly. He packed his few things together quickly, neatly. He kissed Emily on her cheek, touching her shoulder as he reached towards her.

'Come again,' she said lightly.

'As if,' he said. Imitating someone he had heard say that.

They walked through to the kitchen where Meg stood ready to leave. 'One of these days I'll be on time,' she joked, ran her hand across the side of her hair, said, 'Another week like this and I'm out!'

The boy waving from the car, and the quick beep on the horn as Meg raised her eyebrows and puckered her mouth, her frantic Friday face.

Emily locked the back door and drew the bolt that had been there since her own parents' time. Barry had reminded her, twice in just the past few weeks, to make sure she was 'barricaded in' the minute she was there by herself. There'd been a distinct demographic shift, he explained to her. Prices may have been leap-frogging but clientele, especially this side of the motorway, had changed. Was changing all the time. As if he were instructing a child on how the world out there was a big unknown. He told her just take a look next time she was out driving. 'Amazing,' he said, 'once you pay *attention*.' If only she'd sold up a couple of years back when he first suggested it. The tide creeps and you hardly notice and then it's caught up with you. Next thing, the break-in and vandalism quotient has suddenly escalated. 'You'd still do well if you decided to up sticks, Em. It's not the neighbourhood you and Alan used to live in. Not that I'm judgemental either but it's a thing to be aware of.'

It amused her that it was Barry who fired the real estate bullets. Meg presumably thought it wasn't her place to lean on her own mother, beyond her saying once, 'If you ever did decide on moving, mind you, you'd do pretty well.' How considerately, Emily thought, my flesh and blood put things! 'When your fucking number's up', as her own father would bluntly have phrased it. An educated man, her own mother had said, but the tongue on him! It's the army, she had said, trying to defend him. You don't go to a war and come back without some damage done. As if he gave a damn how he put things, as long as he was back, but her mother hated it. Language, as she called it.

Emily went back into the lounge and sat in the chair Donald so liked, without switching on the tall lamp beside it. Now that she was thinking back, don't expect profundity! The turns life takes, she thought. Her mother was a snob for one reason and her daughter a snob for another. 'Mother', as she had insisted on being called once she and Deb were old enough to be aware that how one put things most certainly did matter. Words, Mother said, were little detonations that told you where boundaries lay. And now Meg the bracket on the other side. 'Schools *do* matter!', almost shouting it at her when they had argued about where Donny would have the chance—can't she see that?—to grow up with kids who had the same values. 'You want to bring politics into everything!'

'You want fences around life,' Emily had come back at her. 'That's another way of saying ghetto.'

As if things had ever been so different. As if generations don't repeat themselves over and over. She thought of her own mother's obsession with drawing that big bolt each night, her removing the key from the lock above it and reaching up to place it on the high mantelpiece. There was always someone to keep out. She remembered the war when she was a child and her father had been away, and her mother would say if the Japs ever get here, we'll know about it then all right. Rice paddies as far as Taupō.

Next morning when she woke the room was chilly and the curtains still not drawn. Alan wouldn't have liked to know she was careless about that. The little changes before you noticed, as he liked to say. You have to watch these things, Em. His own problems already setting in, but neither had yet become alert to them. She walked through to the kitchen. The red glare on the bench where her daughter had placed the poinsettia, a thank you for having Donald after school. A different little gift each week. 'No one takes you for granted, Mum.' Ugly damned things they are, however much you crack them up. Those broad, rough dog-tongue leaves. Americans apparently couldn't do without every home having one at Christmas. She could see Meg in one of her rushes, braking in the New World carpark, dashing into the floral arrangements section, declaring 'That one's perfect!' to the woman at the counter, no, no need to wrap it, truly. God, just look at her watch, as if she needed this as well! 'She wouldn't mind,' Donald said to her, 'if you didn't bring something—Em says that every week.' As if we wouldn't, his mother telling him.

She took the plant and its green plastic saucer and placed it on the old plush cloth that covered the oval table that had been there, with that very cover, since she was a child, since before the house became hers and Alan's. The years she had sat at it, reading, sewing, just running her hand back and forth across the dark plush, its faded brocade border falling at the table's sides. She glanced at the calendar above the alcove where the phone sat in a little blue plastic armchair. Meg's presents didn't draw the line at kitsch. The next time the boy was here would be the week before Easter, so no doubt an Easter egg the size of a pumpkin would be the gift of the week. Easter itself of course Donald and his parents would be across in Sydney. My God, as Meg would laugh, if ever there was my kind of town! There would be a card with the Easter egg that said, as her cards often did, 'What would we do without you?!!!' Too early to say, Emily had thought.

Criminal, she thought, the way prices kept jumping week by week, as she took the pinot gris from the fridge. It wasn't as if Meg hadn't said to her, and Barry too, for God's sake, Mother, there's no need to *stint* with anything. As if they'd see her measuring out Villa Maria when there were cartons, as Barry teased her, *cartons* of Te Mata if she'd swallow her pride. What I'd prefer, she had thought, *really* prefer, if I had any say in it, is that you were a different person, Barry, entirely. Or that I was, for as long as I had to listen to you.

Young Donald. Strange how the boy was on her mind so much. He made her think of a fledging perched on the rim of a nest. His school blazer with its pointy bishop's hat, its Latin motto with expensive words such as 'victus' and 'aurum'. All that boys aspire to because they're told to, all we reprimand ourselves for not quite achieving. Amazing, Emily though, the clarity that arrives at the end of the second glass!

She ran her hand over the faded plush she had stroked for as long as she remembered. Her mother, too, with a cloth not so very different from this one. Her fingers pressed for a moment at the hem of thick brocade. She recalled the game with her fat small hands as a child—how she'd hated that word *fat* when anyone else said it—lying across her mother's fingers which were so much longer and nicer than her own, with her rings that didn't come off unless she put soap on her fingers first. But then why would she want to? she said. Ever want to take them off?

Emily liked to think of the past because you could not mess around with it. You could not be sentimental about something set hard as stone. This is what it was, the stones said: you can walk among them if you like but you'll never change a thing. She disliked the way some of her friends spoke of years back as though it were some great chunk of blancmange, where you dipped your spoon and tasted just what you wanted to taste. You couldn't alter a thing: that is what she liked about it. Memory was Stonehenge from a choice of angles. It was there and you were here. You could look at it as long as you liked and imagine it looked back, but the terms were implacable. You took it for what it was, or not at all. The exhilaration, if you had the nerve to face it, of knowing exactly what you were. We know when we're tarting it up, putting a spin on things. But once we get it straight—it's where we sit in judgement on ourselves. It's not always so bad.

Her mother with her gift for fantasy, for her children always brighter in her mind than they were in anyone else's, her saying, refusing to say alcohol, to blame the piss, as her husband frankly did: 'The War of course was what came between us.' Unable to bring herself to say that they were never suited, before the war was even thought of. Mother's fingers stroking the table, year after year. Where Emily too had lain her head, forty years ago and more, her cheek against the flatness of the table, her own body too drunk to move except with effort, yet her mind cold and clear and merciless, the night after her abortion, the gift of refusing to excuse herself, *whatever*. The solace and disgust of drunkenness, the first and only time in her life. The relief and the horror, because indeed there were both.

The summer after her mother had died and life was hers entirely, that too for the first time. Alan back from Vietnam. God knows how they had got over that. Alan in the army and her in love with him and yet marching, shouting, 'Troops out now!' at the American Embassy gates in Thorndon. But in love and knowing they could get over anything! Alan, who was mild and considerate and who ten years later she betrayed in this very kitchen, this same spread velvet cloth beneath her cheek, but this time sober and as unconfused as she had ever been. Her sister in another city, Meg with relatives, the girl's first holiday apart from her, on a farm at Taupiri. A year after her husband's mind had begun to slip while his body, for all you could tell by looking at it, as much the man as it had ever been, that of the man she had loved, and now feared to be with.

Look at the past, Emily reminded herself, so it has to look back. The evening when Deb's husband had picked her up from the Home, where Alan was past speaking for himself. Her sister out of town at one of her Zonta meetings, or whatever. Dan picking her up because her own car had packed up that afternoon. He had driven her home, and she had said, as she did so many times across the years, 'You must have a cup of tea, at least.' The irony of a phrase one does not forget. At least.

Emily removed the poinsettia from where Meg had placed it on the bench, with the card's inanely smiley face. She made a coffee at the gleaming machine Meg and Barry had given her the Christmas before. It hissed and blew like some kind of metal beast, but the coffee was worth it. As good as the advertising promised. Can't imagine life without one of these, Barry had said to her. Nor could she, a few months later, that was the joke of it. She took the big red Avezza mug back to the table. Without noticing it at first, her hand back to its stroking, the nap slightly resisting one way, flowing with the brush of her skin the other. Her own hand. Her mother's.

As she supposed she had done, that evening. 'Hits the spot,' Dan had said, taking the tea from her. He had put his key-ring, attached to its blob of Baltic amber the size of a bumblebee, beside the fern with its wire-thin extensions, its tiny leaves. Her mother too had kept ferns like that on the table for years. Emily supposed she persisted with them because of that. She did not in fact greatly care for them, their fussy delicacy, their air of pay-me-attention, above the hammered copper pot they stood in, the one thing her father lugged back from Cairo. Dan's keys chinking against the metal as he let them fall.

He sat there, Dan her brother-in-law, laughing at something she must have said, and then his leaning back, eyes closed, his head against the wall behind him.

'When's Deb back then?' she asked him. Trying not to convey condescension as she thought of her sister in Wellington for her Helena Rubinstein makeup course, some new scheme for selling not quite door to door, but beyond the confines of department stores and their redolent counters and young bright assistants. Her sister later explained to her how the visiting Australian representative's newsletter sensibly pointed out that women with the time and energy to care about their appearance would prefer to speak with another *grown-up*, and not in the glare of a shop, for heaven's sake! So that's where she was. Receiving tasteful advice in discreet surroundings.

'Back tomorrow,' Dan said. 'Late.'

Then everything happening within seconds, as she thought of it later, yet that could not quite have been so. As if life had become the sudden whirl of a washing machine. As if there was any rational way to think of it, speak of it, that was not a cliché, a banality, a way of excusing where even the word excuse could claim no place.

She had sat at the table, Dan on the small settee facing her, relaxed, talking politics, which he seldom did at home, dipping gingernuts into his tea. They enjoyed chatting together. She knew he would want a second cup. She went through to the kitchen to flick the switch. She saw him raise the sleeve of his jacket and check his watch. Always it had been like this between them, since Deb had first brought him home, tall and considerate, and her parents falling for him as they never had done for Alan, 'holding their counsel', in one of her father's slightly pompous phrases, about a man who served in the army *as a job*. Dan had been nice to her, the older sister, in those years of obsession, as Emily always thought it, when he 'danced attendance'—her mother's phrase, that one—on Deb, who accepted it as her due. Vapid, chattering Deb. So that was what romance was like! As her father used to say, in those early days, it was as good as going to the movies just to see them playing at lovers. Odd that she was thinking of that now, as Dan kept talking across from where she sat. She thought of Alan's rather unkind amusement when 'the colours began to fade', Dan absorbed in his travel business, long before Deb in her gift for advising the mature woman.

She had turned on the kitchen radio before returning with the fresh tea. Something nice, please, she thought as she set the volume to a pleasant background level. Something baroque came through, calming and moderato. Formal and patterned and light, a kind of benign brocade. Her mind oddly noting such things, as she thought too how strange, as if she and Dan hadn't known each other for decades, and yet this feeling as though she must keep a stranger entertained.

'That's nice,' Dan said.

'Dreadful how we so use music for background,' she said. 'I have it on the YC station most of the time. Then ask me at the end of the day what I've listened to and I doubt I could tell you even one piece.'

'Filling in time,' Dan said. 'When it comes down to it, that's what most of our lives are about.'

His surprising her, saying that.

'Well, tea helps, to be profound about it.' She placed the cup and saucer on a low table beside him. Her hair brushed against him as she leaned forward, and quickly drew back.

'You're right there,' Dan said. Each of them taking refuge, Emily would later think, in whatever cliché came to hand. He was talking about his recent visit to the capital. The bad name it had for weather, and so deserved.

Crossing back to the table she saw how the plush cover had ruckled up on the far side. Like her mother in that too, she supposed, her liking things to stay tidy, stay smooth, the little habits that keep us going. She leaned across, settling the cloth ahead of her with her arms at full stretch, her heels slipping up from her flat shoes as she pressed forward against the table's edge, her calves taut with the rise. For a second there her body arcing forward, a diver ready to take off.

A mistake, as she would think of it later. No point looking for reasons, yet how one's mind goes over things! Her fingers fitting the cloth back down between the table and the wall, her knuckles against the chalky brush of the wallpaper, when she felt the hands set against the outside of her thighs, the coolness of the air against her suddenly exposed skin as her skirt was raised. Roughly? Gently? She had no idea. Knowing only she had been driven forward, her face turned and her cheek against the cloth's smoothness, the irrational and even demented fact—so it would come to seem—that this was not a surprise, still less an assault. A muddle that was never quite to be untangled. *I let it happen and neither then nor now do I know if I regret it.* Her bare feet now planted level on the floor. Her pressing back against him. To comply. As though it were a fragment of time from other lives, but not their own. She would have no real notion of what he thought, of whether her brother-in-law, who deceived her sister, might feel guilt or elation or indifference—how does one presume to guess? *Momentary*. Beyond the vagueness of that, what certainty, even in herself?

The absurdity of it, that too, the grotesque and comic sprawl they would have seen had a film later revealed it to them, the copper pot of maidenhair fern rocking in its clay saucer, the plant's bouncing droop like a green claw dabbing down on her head, the rasp of Dan's breath and the sustained lurching of the table, and beyond that the *silence* that was there across them, like a canopy, the word that stayed with her, and the *unlikeliness*—what did this have to do with either of them? The bruise from his impacting belt against her rump. And no memory, even a week later, of what might have been said, or if they spoke at all, as they then put themselves together—what a phrase! Drawing themselves back to where the world, to call it that, had been ten minutes before.

It was several months until she saw her brother-in-law again, at her father's funeral. Dan stood beside his wife and his arm lay beneath hers as she stooped to take up a clutch of earth and lean forward to release it into the grave. Then the banal but piercing shimmer, as it always struck her, of the bugle at the end of the prayers, and the undertaker deftly removing the flag from the coffin before it was lowered. Stagey, moving, as it always was. Emily stood with a group of relatives and friends. Mostly old people. Younger than she was now, as she thought of it, her fingers beside the box where the boy so neatly stacked away the red and black pieces of their game.

These splinters, she thought, these fragments of history, of what is really oneself. Yet almost everything a little trivial across time, which perhaps is what perspective comes to mean. If you looked closely at the faded cloth her hand returned to you could make out that once its pattern had been globed nectarines and sprays of curving leaves, although you would hardly guess at them now. How once they must have been.

'What's making you laugh?' Donald asked her. Their usual Friday evening. Their eating the omelette she always made for him and then the things cleared away and the pieces set out on the board, their clatter together as they poured from the box, clack-clacking on each other. 'You're always doing that. Laughing at me.'

'The way you think every game you can beat me,' Emily said. 'I don't know why you don't just give up.'

His knowing she was teasing him. He didn't mind but sometimes he wished she would see he only beat her because he was getting better at it every week. He wished too that Mum would lay off thinking she had to remind him to watch his manners, to remember his grandmother was old and not to tire her, that you had to be nice to them, old people.

'I *like* going there.' He had told her that enough, you'd think she'd know.

'Of course you do,' his father would say. 'Like Fergus likes being put in his crate when we all go out.'

'Give it a rest,' his mother was likely to say when his father said things like that. Sometimes when they picked him up later on they wouldn't say a word until they were home. Then talking too loudly downstairs and Mum making sure his bedroom door was closed. He wouldn't mind being at Emily's a lot more than just Friday nights, as if he hadn't told them that. Of course other Fridays it wasn't like that at all. They would laugh and all when they got back home, they'd put music on, you'd think it was a party if you can say a party with just two people.

These last few weeks Donald had been on about the war, the one a hundred years ago. They had gone from school in a bus to see an exhibition. Guns, he told Emily, old trucks and things, an aeroplane made out of cardboard and stuff. Real blood, it looked like real blood on the make-believe faces and that.

Like really dead. The teacher and another man explained things. Why the kings were fighting, although each country had its own special word for king. 'And you couldn't get out of it,' Donald told her. 'You just had to go because your country needed you.' He liked coming back to the planes. 'Did you know they only had stuff on the wings like, you know, *stuff*. Canvas or something?'

'I know, they were a bit like boxes,' Emily told him. She scooped the pieces together. 'You set the pieces this time so I can beat you again.'

'And if you dropped a bomb you just leaned over like this,' the boy said, leaning out from the table, ready to drop one on the carpet. 'You just let it go.'

Meg had warned her there'd be little else but war talk. She had no idea, her daughter said, why they so hammered the whole damned business of it even with the tiny kids. To think there were years of it before the bloody commemorations were over!

Then Emily suddenly remembered them. She knew Meg would be enraged. She went through to the bedroom and opened the top drawer of the tallboy, where Alan had kept his cheque book and passport and odds and end. It was pretty much as he had left it. She took the two medals from the box he had never removed them from. Surprising how heavy they were, and how fresh, how brightly their ribbons flared in the light from above the table. 'You might as well wear these,' she said, 'while you try to win against me.' And then, 'They were Grand-dad's.'

The boy was beside himself. His fingers ran across the crinkled material of the ribbons and the patterns on the cast metal discs. She helped him pin them on his school jersey.

He played now with a new seriousness, and Emily guessed what was in his mind, as he hesitated, revised his move, clicked with his tongue as his tanks moved across the board to annihilate her own. And after their engagements were over, she told him, 'I don't think you should take them home, they're so easy to lose. Although they're really yours. I'll just keep them here for you until you're older.'

'When you're dead?' Donald said.

Emily liked to think how his mother would have spoken in that tiresome instructive way of hers when instilling the kind of things you must and mustn't say if you wanted people to like you. 'And we want people to like us, don't we?', the flourish she tended to conclude with.

'Sooner than that. Once you're old enough.'

She guessed the boy was calculating his chances.

Then, 'What did they do,' he asked her, jumping back to tactical matters, 'after things were bombed?'

'Made them over again, I suppose. Put the lost things back.'

'To look the same?'

'If they could.'

'So a room like this would stay the same?'

'Pretty much.'

Strange, how saying something so simple moved her. She put one hand across the other, to hold it still, while Donald set up the pieces for what would be their last game before the lights swept across the windows as the car drove up, and his mother would fling in at the door, telling him to get a move on, you know how Dad hates waiting.

'I'm black this time,' he said. He tapped one of the pieces on the board, to warn her he was ready. His fingers came up and touched the medals.

'This time you're for it, Emily,' he said. The severe voice he used with her when there were still games to win. 'I mean, really for it.' He moved the first of his pieces forward to where her own, more threatening than ever, were lined up and waiting.

'Not a chance,' she told him.

JOHANNA AITCHISON

Anna & the Monster Lake

Anna walks along the beach teeth, sits down
against the tree beside the DANGER cliff.

There are rocks on yellow, signs of stickmen
missing cliffs & flying, finally.

Anna is watching the bark-off boats
stir up the evening.

Anna is watching the cloth couple
uncover their bones & walk into the bruise.

Anna is watching the woman
in a scream bikini.

LEONARD LAMBERT

Nights of Wonder, Days of Splendour

These hot-water bottles have had it, you said,
we need new ones.
So I placed them in the bin
with slightly more care than called for
and was suddenly shocked by what I saw,
ashamed at what I'd done.
It was the covers, soft and woollen,
which lay there like two lovers.
These had known our bodies, our blood, secret things—
surely they must stay. Okay, you said,
and with new bottles oldly clad
we grinned at each other, absurdly glad—

Nights of wonder, days of splendour

—lovers are mad.

ELIZABETH SMITHER

The Ten Conductors

The conductor had given his permission and now Jacqueline was seated in the second row of the orchestra, beside her friend Evelyn, the second clarinet. Behind her right shoulder was a screen like an old-fashioned fireguard to protect her from the sound of the horns and trumpets and trombones. She was inside a forest of music stands with sheet music that threatened to levitate each time the doors of the gymnasium opened and another member of the orchestra hurried in. The conductor was sitting on the edge of the stage, consulting his watch. He reminded her of Sam, the American bald eagle in *The Muppet Show*: a fierce unyielding look. Evelyn had told her he could detect a bum note and single out the culprit. And now he was rising to his feet, taking up his position, tapping on the edge of the podium with his baton.

Jacqueline had always wondered what it would be like to be in the middle of an orchestra during a performance. Would it be like a forest through which a sighing wind moved? Or a sea whose movement came from the depths until the surface broke in a spray of notes? Evelyn had explained how important it was to count the bars, not to lose one's place. Then it truly would be a forest, the breadcrumbs dropped by Hansel and Gretel scooped up by birds, and the conductor swooping overhead with outstretched wings.

Jacqueline was invited for the morning. In the afternoon there was a troublesome Bruckner symphony. By then the conductor's patience might have worn thin at the sight of an imposter behind an empty music stand.

As a child Jacqueline had learnt piano. Her parents bought a neat upright in dark mahogany which her mother discovered later had a wooden not an iron frame. When it was sold a few years later much was made of its immaculate appearance. Jacqueline learnt a few pieces: *Rustle of Spring*, Mozart's Sonata in C major, *Für Elise*, a John Field nocturne. Somehow she could never get her feelings to reach to her fingertips, to convey those feelings to the keys. She had a gift for theory and had passed a few exams. Details overcame her: the pressing down of a white key, the stroking (for it felt different) of a black key. She could lose herself in a sensation and forget the music's onward movement. 'We gave her the chance,' her parents said the day the sale went through.

By accident she heard Enesco's Rumanian Rhapsody no. 1 on Concert FM. She saved part of her salary—she was working in a bank—and ordered the record from HMV. It was a Friday night and the shop was softly lit and the turntable was playing *Fly Robin Fly*. She played Enesco at full volume until the windows of her flat rattled and someone tapped on the wall. Whenever she found a piece of music she liked she played it over and over. If she heard Enesco's Rumanian Rhapsody today she would wince. Its contribution became a dislike for music that held back its themes, whispered them at the beginning and then allowed them to swell at the end. Mozart she loved for his prodigal inventiveness as he navigated through the galaxies in a silver spaceship. After Enesco came Beethoven's Ninth. She leaned on the counter at HMV and the same assistant served her. 'Toscanini,' he said. 'Take my word for it. No one else comes close.' He went off to serve another customer, then came back. 'Arturo will make you pace the room,' he said. 'I guarantee it.' Jacqueline's flat was not very large. Nonetheless she was persuaded. Eventually Toscanini's treatment of the choir began to seem sadistic and she only played the first three movements.

She thought of this when Sam Eagle raised his baton and seemed to fix his gaze on her. It was the middle distance, not her personally, she told herself. She lowered her eyes as a critic in the front row of a theatre might. Beside her she could feel Evelyn's body tense. In the final seconds her fingers had reached to press down the fold on the second and fourth pages of the score. Above each bar was a clearly pencilled number.

Jacqueline visualised the sound travelling like an arrowhead towards the conductor. Not only did he have to beat time but he had to adjudicate whether the cellos were too dominant or not dominant enough, whether the first and second violins were balanced, whether the horns came in at the right time. The horns were behind her and at their first blast she leapt in her seat as if she had been stabbed. Evelyn caught her eye and smiled but it was for the briefest time; her eyes quickly returned to the score. How could anyone survive in such a cacophony? And this was just a little orchestra; if they played a large work, musicians were brought in from other orchestras. Evelyn would be joined by another clarinet, there would be more woodwinds, an extra timpanist. How would it be in the middle of the Berlin Philharmonic, the London Symphony Orchestra, the Concertgebouw? What a frighteningly dark forest that must be.

Jacqueline's ears were buzzing. She fought the impulse to cover them with her hands; kept her head lowered. Evelyn's face was lost to her, in deep concentration. And this concentration did not lapse when a few bars signified a rest. If anything it grew more intense, like someone taking a deep breath in preparation for another foray. An archer cowering from a hail of arrows, relieved that his shield had held and his chainmail was unbreached. The trumpets and horns and bassoons cleared the moisture from their instruments and seemed to sit up straighter.

Der Freischütz seemed to both be constructed and fall apart before her ears. Obviously it was meant to galvanise and impress, to hush an audience fidgeting in their seats. Then, once the audience's attention was gained, a little levity was allowed but always the sense of hurrying like a flowing river or rushing air on a mountain top. Tunes were embedded within it—tunes that might be sung or whistled in the street. The end came with a huge chord like an animal's pelt being nailed to a wall and she wanted to leap out of her chair and run for the door. Instead she touched Evelyn's arm with her hand, hoping her face expressed excitement and awe.

The orchestra broke for morning tea: tea or coffee and fresh-baked scones. A few players went outside to smoke. The gym doors were flung open to admit the cold air and then hastily closed.

'Should I say something to the conductor?' Jacqueline asked. 'Introduce myself?'

'I think we'll leave him,' Evelyn said. 'Perhaps when the rehearsal is over.'

'I'm not sure I can stay for the afternoon.'

'You'll miss the Bruckner.'

'The one that sounds like bears growling? I should certainly like to hear that.'

She was being half-truthful. Growling bears might be all right, the heavy moodiness less so.

They took their seats again and this time she straightened her back and squared her shoulders. She caught the conductor's eye and gave a small nod. She would send a card, something with a musical motif.

She would tell people she had sat in on an orchestra rehearsal. 'Literally *inside* the orchestra.' She would explain the conductor was like a policeman, regulating the sounds before they sped into the stalls and balconies and circle and found their perfect balance, ironically, in the hard, backless seats of the gods. When the doors to the gods opened there was a rush and a tumbling forward to reach the front row where you could rest your arms on the edge of the balcony and see into the wings where the musicians were forming up. There were little gestures carried only to the gods: someone might adjust a cummerbund or dust a shoulder sprinkled with dandruff.

The performance in three weeks' time would be in the Opera House with its scarlet and gold boxes newly restored; its chandeliers freshly washed. Ushers in black skirts and white blouses would lead the audience down vacuumed aisles to their seats of yellow plush.

Jacqueline darted a glance at Sam Eagle and thought he looked worried. Perhaps he was worrying about the orchestra's varying degrees of amateurism. The woman who baked a fruit cake for each rehearsal and played too loudly. The elderly male violinist who hardly moved his arms, in contrast to the two students fresh from high school who made baroque gestures with their bows. Yet despite these disparities it was an orchestra with charm. Charm was hardly the word to describe the Vienna Philharmonic or the LSO. Orchestras whose bows rose in such synchronicity they resembled trees of uniform height, and whose horns, bassoons, flutes and timpani seemed to ration their effects, such was their control.

But this little orchestra had endearing moments when it sometimes got lost in the dark wood of Beethoven or Brahms, when an informed listener might say 'Surely this is not Beethoven's Seventh?' But then, miraculously, it would right itself. The leading violin would pull them back, the conductor would coax them back onto safe ground. The applause and the bows would come as usual—sometimes there might be a sheepish look, quickly masked but many in the audience, drowning in the last chords, were unaware. If Evelyn was playing, Jacqueline would not mention this unless her friend raised it first. And then she would speak admiringly of the regaining of control. 'Those few bars still contained some Beethoven, like sugar crystals in the bottom of a cup. He wasn't totally forgotten.' She was careful to choose her words because no clarinet had been at fault and she didn't know whether her friend was disappointed or not.

Furtwängler, Herbert von Karajan, Leopold Stokowski: Jacqueline counted their names. She dismissed Sir Henry Wood, whose benign bust presided over the Proms. The tiger conductors, the panthers. The ones who were hardly contained by the podium on which they rose on their arches, tailcoats flying, shoulders threatening to rise to the level of their ears, brows dripping until a white handkerchief might be produced, like Pavarotti. Eventually the heyday of the tigers and panthers passed. Orchestras stopped trembling at the appearance of the conductor; at rehearsals players' views were sought, other interpretations tried. No longer was there dread of beetling brows or sighs that carried to the timpani and double basses. Yet Jacqueline always chose those names first. How suited they were to Wagner or Mahler. Audiences loved them: Sir Thomas Beecham's rapier wit, Herbert von Karajan in a tailcoat lined with leopard spots, Furtwängler declining to shake the hand of Hitler.

The tea break was coming to an end when Jacqueline turned to Evelyn and made her excuses. She couldn't hear her own voice because her ears were buzzing. Then, with a final hug, she turned and walked to the door. But either she was not walking quite straight or the floorboards were shifting. She could hear voices around her, pages rustling, teaspoons touching the sides of cups. Her car was parked alongside a flowerbed but the flowers were blurred. She backed out carefully and drove over the cattlestop by the school gates, then through the quiet suburbs to the main road. She had gone through two sets of traffic lights before the buzzing stopped. The Chicago Symphony, the Orchestra of the Age of Enlightenment—how do they stand it? They must all be profoundly deaf. At each concert they must be lost as well as deaf. She saw them in their tailcoats, long black skirts and evening dresses resembling moles, blindly bending over bows, blowing into mouthpieces, clashing cymbals. And the conductor, as the sound travelled towards and then past him, leading them on.

On the night of the performance Jacqueline sits with friends in one of the boxes. She can look down on the clarinets and bassoons. Evelyn looks up and Jacqueline waves but she can tell she is elsewhere, already entering mole territory, absorbed by notes heard and unheard. She wonders if there is a thesis to be written about changes in society synonymous with the changing mindsets of the great conductors. Quite often she listens to a conductor being interviewed during an intermission at Carnegie Hall. None are bombastic; all talk of the merits of the orchestra over which they had a brief tenure. At the end of a concert the most peremptory gesture is when the conductor compels a section of the orchestra to stand. The most prominent goes first—the brass perhaps, or the trumpets, the cellos who played in unison, the forest of violins.

This sets wave after wave of applause rolling in and soon there are bouquets, which the announcer describes—blue irises for Giordano Bellincampi or white lilies for Renée Fleming. Sometimes, in fact quite often, these bouquets are handed to a member of the orchestra who is retiring, or even a member of the audience, who has risen from the front row of the stalls in shock and excitement.

Jacqueline drove to Locals café, where she and Evelyn were meeting for lunch. The café was started by a woman who loved baking and its reputation had spread. The large room was almost full and she went in search of a table on which to put her library books and jacket. She found one on a little raised dais.

'I'm going to give up orchestra,' Evelyn said when their coffees and cakes arrived. 'It's taking up too much time.'

Frivolously, Jacqueline thought of Alice and the Mad Hatter. 'But you are so good at time,' she told her friend.

'It's the rehearsals. There's an extra practice this week and now the pianist who is playing Rachmaninov has had to cancel and that's been rescheduled. Sometimes I feel I hate music.'

Jacqueline put her spoon back in the saucer. She had been lifting the layer of chocolate-flecked foam, decorated with a fern, to her mouth. She placed her hand on Evelyn's. She felt she had been unsympathetic. There was no payment for rehearsals except for cups of tea and home baking, of variable quality. She remembered a New Zealand Symphony Orchestra concert at the Michael Fowler Centre where she had fastened her eyes on a woman in the first violins. The woman had an exquisite profile that seemed to have been worn down by music. A noble forehead, a shapely nose, cheekbones that a model might envy. It was only when the orchestra stood to take a bow and the woman turned face on that Jacqueline saw she was not young and the opposite profile had a more worried look, as if she were thinking of bills and food on the table.

At the door of the café they hugged. Music was essential but its creation was not always without pain. Her nose got entangled in Evelyn's black and white scarf with bass and treble clefs.

It was amazing how long conductors lived. Was it all the shoulder and foot work, the raising of calf muscles, the little dances atop the podium? No need to go to a gym or use an exercycle. (Actually a von Karajan or a Bernstein might well have a private gym, or cycle for miles before a concert. Perhaps from Rome to Paris or New York to Toronto.) Then there was the workout for the shoulders, the arms, the fingers. A protective wife might learn massage or hire a masseur. One built like a tank who could prod and pummel. Then the trophy wife would bring a cocktail and whisper endearments in his ear.

But how could you tame a wild animal? *The conductor is receiving a bouquet of orchids and roses which he has impulsively awarded to a woman in the front row*, the Concert FM host is saying. The conductor's wife might be displeased if he chose a woman in a strapless gown. Bruno Walter, Leopold Stokowski, Jacqueline listed more names to herself. She wanted to reach ten, and so far she had seven. She wracked her brain for the remaining three. Not Neville Marriner, whom she imagined to be tame. Sir Neville Marriner and the Orchestra of St Martin in the Fields. Though there were no fields, just an old worn-down church with a crypt where the homeless bedded down and an army of volunteers made soup and sandwiches. There were bodies sleeping in the doorways when Jacqueline walked past on her first visit to London. She had heard it was safer to sleep in the daytime. She had stopped and put a few coins in a cup by one of the mattresses. No flicker of the eyelids to show the sleeper was aware of her presence. That might be a protective measure as well, she thought, walking on and crossing at the lights, still regretting that the fields were gone like the fields around Keats' house. If she could just master the list of Ten Fearsome Conductors she might start another list of Ten Gentle Conductors. Just as she was turning into her driveway the final three rushed at her, like three fierce hounds. Otto Klemperer, Fritz Reiner, Hector Berlioz.

Evelyn was as good as her word and gave up the orchestra. There was an attempt at bargaining but she was determined to play just for her own pleasure. Her husband and grown-up children would hear her playing and she would play to her grandchildren. She would stand at the French doors and play to her garden, to the little yew hedge, to the tulip tree that had been festooned with cards and ribbons and paper hearts for her daughter's wedding. This was the playing she had always liked best. Did the Albertine rose incline towards the sound of the clarinet, did it grow faster than the sweetheart rose on the far side of the garden?

Her little dog, Barkley, lay at her feet, looking up at the music stand which had been a parting gift from the orchestra. Sam Eagle had said she would be missed, despite occasionally misplaying a note. Evelyn had laughed but she was relieved when she could leave with her clarinet case in one hand and a bunch of stargazer lilies in the other. 'Sleep,' she said to the clarinet as she laid it on the passenger seat. Its case was lined with green panne velvet, grown shabby over the years. All she wanted was to go to sleep but instead she lay awake most of the night, going over pieces she had played, some easily and with confidence and others that had had her practising in the dawn when everyone else was asleep, even Barkley, who spent his nights on the sofa. Sam Eagle seemed to recognise this extra devotion for he sometimes raised an eyebrow at her or said a quiet word during the break.

'I hate Holst,' she had confessed to him once. She knew that Holst was a self-effacing man who carried oranges in his pocket as he walked around Hammersmith, looking at the Thames. Just before she fell asleep a poem saved her—

the river glideth at his own sweet will:
Dear God! The very houses seem asleep
And all that mighty heart is lying still.

Winter came and there were two orchestra concerts. A visiting pianist played Rachmaninoff's Concerto no. 2, marred only by a small fumble which had the orchestra confused for a few minutes before they were led out by the joint efforts of the conductor and the first violin; and *Carmina Burana*, for which reinforcements were brought in. Jacqueline and Evelyn sat in the front row of the circle, leaning forward and resting their elbows on the plush railing. 'I'm out of it now,' Evelyn said as they took the lift with its glassed-in sides to the ground floor. Jacqueline noticed that Evelyn was greeted by several members of the orchestra, who were all going to the conductor's house for supper.

'Do you miss it?' Jacqueline asked when they were walking briskly through the cold air towards a bar.

'They might have known there was a concert tonight,' Evelyn said as they stood eyeing the meagre offerings in the cabinets. In the end they shared a large slab of carrot cake with thick icing, most of which they left on the plate.

The Opera House as they drove past was deserted, fallen back into that blankness that overcomes theatres and nightclubs, stadiums whose atmosphere must be built from the ground up. Suddenly it seemed to Evelyn like friendship itself. The closed theatre was like those dormant times when the friend was absent and yet the friendship was not inactive. In a few short hours someone would switch on the lights, there would be a phone call, the vibrancy or otherwise of a voice would be judged.

'I often think of the way music ends,' Jacqueline remarked as the dark streets sped past. 'The way the brakes are engaged, the number of blows to the back of the neck, the final chord. Did you think of things like that when you were playing?'

'Not really,' Evelyn replied. 'But I know what you mean. It must be in the conductor's mind: this plane has got to land.'

'Backward thrust,' Jacqueline said. 'That always had something musical about it. Beethoven lands at Gate 25.'

'Whump,' Evelyn said. 'That was always my word for it.'

'Rachmaninoff stamps out the syllables of his name. Rach-man-in-off. Piss off, Rachmaninoff.'

Then, in the silence, Evelyn thought not in terms of an ending, a final chord, but a beginning. That morning Concert FM had been playing Mendelssohn's String symphony no. 2 in D major, written when he was twelve and had been removed from the academy because there was nothing left to teach him.

They were almost at Evelyn's street.

'Ten conductors,' Jacqueline said, looking at her friend sideways. 'Can you name ten conductors? The fierce ones, the tomcats. Not Henry Wood or Neville Marriner. And you have to do it without hesitation.'

'I think I'm too tired,' Evelyn said. 'I'm musicked out. I need a straitjacket and a padded cell.'

'Sam the American Eagle,' Jacqueline said, leaning over to bestow a kiss on her cheek. 'He's the winner tonight.'

She watched her friend walk up the path. Tonight, like her clarinet, she would sleep. A deeper sleep, perhaps. Driving back it struck her that the stars were so unabashed. Whatever moved them, whatever music of the spheres, they needed no respite. They sat on, glittering and overdressed, like the audience in the circle, never needing to leave their seats.

CILLA MCQUEEN

Adaptation

Found on the beach—is it a fossil?
jawbone? hunk of coral?
Fire-blackened fragment of Janola bottle,
contorted plastic colonised by weeds
and sandy encrustations, printed instructions
still visible here and there, pale blue.
Growing inside the intact neck, poking out
like a pearly beak, a baby oyster.

PIP ROBERTSON

Disaster Day

My son claims he wants to swim. This afternoon on the way to the pool, he said today was the day he would do it for real. He says that every time. It's when he sees the water that he baulks.

He scrabbles and clings to me, even in the shallows. A lifeguard came up to us last week and said she was sorry, but I had to leave the pool. I thought it was because of the scene my son was making, but she pointed to the back of my arm. His fingernails had left a long scratch and my arm was smeared with blood.

He didn't come close to drawing blood today. He wouldn't even let go of the side.

'If I start drowning, could you save me?'

'You won't drown. It isn't deep and there are lifeguards.'

'But could you do it? Could you save me?'

I told my son that yes, I could save him.

I used to work in an office where someone had died of a heart attack during a budget meeting. It wasn't like everyone just stood around and watched, but an inquiry found that more could have been done, and we all had to attend a CPR course.

I don't remember the ratio of breaths to compressions. We practised that on a head and torso model, and swabbed its rubbery mouth with alcohol between turns. I do remember the recovery position. We needed arms and legs for that, so practised on each other. People could opt out if they didn't feel comfortable. I didn't feel comfortable, but also didn't feel comfortable voicing my discomfort, and so lay down and shut my eyes as a colleague I didn't know well gently arranged my limbs.

Later in the morning the instructor had shown us how to resuscitate a baby. Back then, having a child of my own seemed so far off it was like walking on the moon—technically possible, but hardly likely.

'How was Disaster Day?' I asked my son on the way home from the pool.

At school they had run through all the emergency drills: fire, earthquake, tsunami, shooter. The notice sent to parents about Disaster Day had said they aimed to keep the activities light and positive, and encouraged us to talk about our children's experiences and reinforce safety messages afterwards.

'All right,' he said and looked out the car window.

I didn't push it.

Nothing has worked. We have offered rewards, withheld rewards, told him no with unwavering consistency. We have tried night lights, a heater, an open window, white noise. Ignored him when he yelled. Yelled back. Held the door handle as he wrenched on it, screaming and kicking. Kept holding it as his sobs turned to coughs that sounded like he couldn't breathe until eventually he was sick.

A friend said, 'You can't keep letting him win.' But if that was winning, don't show me his losing state.

And so I lie on the bed with him every night until he is in a deep enough state of sleep that I can leave. And it must be me, not my husband. My son says that I am the only one who knows how to make him sleep, and it is impossible if I'm not there.

'But I don't do anything. I just lie here.'

'That's what I mean.'

His sleep never lasts long in his own bed. Some time between midnight and two, he wakes inconsolable. He blunders down the hallway to our bedroom and into our bed, where I stroke his head and tell him everything is ok. He doesn't usually wake up again, once he is with us, just thrashes in his sleep like something hooked on a line.

He can never explain what has disturbed him. In the daytime he refuses to acknowledge it even happens. We tell ourselves that he will grow out of it. We have been telling ourselves that for years.

Tonight, after I settled him in his bed, I washed the dishes and listened to a podcast about a suicide cult. I wash dishes by hand, rather than in the dishwasher. This always feels virtuous and satisfying in a way I can't explain.

It ended—the cult, I mean—twenty years ago with a mass intentional drug overdose in a San Diego mansion. I remember it happening, and the news reports that the cult members were wearing matching shrouds and Nike sneakers when they died. Nike stopped making the sneakers after the suicide. I've looked them up online. I figured they'd be a collectors' item by now, and was right. The prices are astronomical.

I was still in the kitchen when my husband came home.

He kissed my head, and started to dry.

'You do know it takes more water to wash them by hand,' he said.

I said I didn't see how that could be true.

He searched for the dishwasher specs on his phone, and showed me.

'Eleven litres for the whole cycle. Ten if it's on the eco-setting.'

He started talking through the calculations on the capacity of the sink, which I usually fill twice, plus the rinsing beforehand.

'You can't talk,' I said. 'You take planes so often you have gold status.'

'That's got nothing to do with dishes. And I travel for work, not by choice. All I'm saying is what you're doing doesn't save time or water.'

'All I'm saying is while we hurtle towards extinction, there are bigger things to worry about than a few litres of water.'

'Why do you always have to go there?'

'Go where?'

'To the end of the world. Sometimes it's impossible to talk about anything without you catastrophising.'

'It's not catastrophising when it is an actual, inevitable, scientifically projected catastrophe.'

It was a stupid argument, interrupted by our son calling out from his bedroom.

I met my husband at university, though we didn't know each other well then. We met again about eight years later, at a boozy dinner party. He had been away: London, then a scholarship at an American university. We ended up back at my place. We lay in the dark talking about people we knew, and where they were now. He remembered me better than I remembered him.

'I was intimidated by you,' he said. 'It was like compared to everyone else you had weightier things on your mind.'

I told him that the weightier thing was probably my weight. The time he was recalling I was constantly preoccupied with calculating the calories of what I had eaten and what I was therefore allowed to eat next. I've never been good at maths and the whole thing was exhausting.

I hadn't admitted that to many people before. In our early time together, talking was a form of undressing, all those layers to reveal and share. And there was the actual undressing, too. It's like we were another species, like we got all our sustenance from sex and conversation.

Imagine having no hunger for sleep.

Sometimes we try to pinpoint what it might be about.

There was the car accident. It was a wet day, and traffic was close and crawling, so when the front car stopped too suddenly and the fifth car stopped too slowly, the four cars in the middle were shunted into each other. Ours was the third car. The driver at the front was furious. He got out of his car, paced back along the queue of cars before anyone else had even processed what was happening. My son had been sleeping in his car seat until the jolt woke him, but he only started to cry when the yelling driver came up to his window. No one was hurt, and the damage was limited to scraped paint and tail lights. For months afterward, whenever we approached that intersection my son would ask if the angry man was still there.

Perhaps it was the storm, when we watched the trees outside bend and spring like they were held together with rubber bands. The morning revealed that the neighbours across the road had lost half their garden to a slip. He kept asking when our garden was going to go, too.

Or perhaps it was a news item that we paused on a moment too long. Perhaps the drowned boy. Or the boy in the camp. Or the boy in the back of the ambulance, freshly dusted with rubble. They were all the same age as my son, give or take.

One of the cult survivors has a voice so hesitant it's as if he is handing you a tiny fragile egg every time he speaks. He says they were all seeking something to give their lives shape and meaning. Death held no fear for them, he says.

He left a few years before the mansion and sneakers.

For years I thought my husband was conscientious. We were at a friend's wedding when I realised he is actually ambitious. And then it was only because someone else pointed it out.

The ceremony was outdoor, the food was vegan, the bride walked down the aisle with her dog. There was an uncle from out of town. He looked puzzled by it all, and I thought my husband was taking pity on him by striking up conversation.

'I don't know where he gets his drive,' a friend said to me, looking over at my husband talking with the uncle.

'Drive?'

'Always looking for opportunities.'

The friend took my confusion for offence.

'Sorry, that came out wrong. It's not a bad thing, I just couldn't do it.'

Soon after that wedding we moved to Singapore. The uncle was a partner in a firm there, and my husband had impressed him enough to get a job offer between canapès.

We were there for four years and I can't say if I liked Singapore. I liked the food, but everyone likes the food. I liked the swimming pool in our apartment complex. We could afford a lifestyle there that we couldn't here, and I didn't vacuum once. But as a place to live, Singapore was at once unfamiliar and unsurprising. There was nothing to spark nostalgia but little to spark curiosity either.

I didn't think that New Zealand was a safer place to raise a child, exactly, but that the hazards seemed more wholesome, more authentic. In Singapore there were no trees to climb and fall from, only concrete ledges. There were rumours of venomous snakes and pythons, but no one I spoke to had actually seen one. In Singapore I only ever felt cool inside buildings, from air conditioning. How could a child be resilient if it only knew cold as something created by a machine?

If it had been up to my husband, we would still be there. No question.

To his credit, he never points that out.

The building I was working in when I did the CPR course was one of the ones condemned after the earthquake last year. From the outside all you could see were some hairline cracks in the concrete but in the right kind of earthquake, the engineer was quoted as saying, the floors could all come down, pancaking one on top of the other.

I took my son to see it being demolished.

Machinery, I thought. Children like machinery.

There was a crowd, and we had to stand back behind barriers.

'Where did you used to sit?' he asked me. It was more than a dozen years since I had left that job, and from the outside I couldn't even be sure which level it had been. But I pointed at one corner. He kept his eyes focused on that spot, and squeezed my hand when the wrecking ball made contact.

'There it goes,' I said, trying to keep my voice bright.

For Disaster Day, the shooter scenario would be that someone believed to possess firearms was on school grounds and making threats, and the armed offenders squad was attending. While unlikely, the notice from school said, a situation like this was unfortunately possible and it was important that the teachers were able to practise a response.

The children would not be told all the details of the scenario.

The older pupils would be told that there was someone in the playground who was upset and needed space and the police were helping them.

The younger pupils would be told that an animal had escaped from the zoo.

The one thing I miss about Singapore is the rain. Humidity built during the day, until even the air was laden and overripe and weighed on you, and then a rainstorm would release the pressure and wash it all down. Or, rather, I miss that feeling in the moments after the rain stops, when it was like everything was given the chance to start over again.

When he was four, my son asked me if we would die.

'Yes,' I said.

'When will it happen?'

And I realised he thought it was something we would do together.

'Not for a long, long time. Not for a hundred birthdays.'

'We get a hundred birthdays!'

At the time, he was delighted by my lie. He's wiser, now.

Sometimes I think about how if he was a different kind of kid, life would be easier. But your brain isn't allowed to get close to these thoughts. It skitters away, like an animal scared of a flame. It's dangerous, and pointless. This is the boy that I have. He falls asleep in the crook of my arm and his trust in me is complete.

I ease myself out of my son's bed once he is asleep enough. I'm as practised and silent as a mime artist. His breath has left a damp patch on my arm.

My husband has gone to bed, and kept a bedside light on for me. I get in and try not to wake him, but he stirs and rolls towards me.

'He's asleep?'

'For now.'

My husband yawns, hugely. 'It's your birthday soon. Is there anything special you'd like?'

'I saw some sneakers online. Vintage.'

'Yeah? You want them?'

I pull his arm around me, lying close while we can. In an hour or two or three our son will be here between us.

'Nah. I'm good.'

STEPHANIE JOHNSON

The Pear Tree

One morning Jena got out of bed and discovered her feet couldn't feel the ground. When she lifted her left leg, bent it at the knee and turned it up at the ankle to press gently into the heel she registered full sensation, likewise along the rest of her sole. Peculiar. She repeated the experiment with her right foot with the same result. The objects on the bedside rug looked smaller. Her jandals could be a half size less. Barbie's head, separated from her body, was more pin-like than ever.

Bend over, examine. The optical illusion was caused by a distance between her feet and the floor, around five centimetres. Later she'd get her tape measure to find out exactly—but at that moment any scientific response was entirely annulled by total panic.

'Jack?'

But in the ensuite the shower ran on, for twenty minutes now, just as it had most mornings since he got the waterproof casing for his phone.

Deep breath. Her reflection in the mirror was higher, her head almost level with the top bar of the frame. When she tried to put her foot down, to insist on getting the balls of her feet on terra firma, there was an answering push back, gentle and firm, like a loving mother saying 'Don't be silly, dear.' This was terrifying. Instinct had her try to step away from herself. The last time she'd done that was when she was in labour with Mitch and she'd decided, deep in her groggy pethidine brain, to go home and get away from the agony. She would like to walk away from this too, but how could it be possible to walk if your feet don't touch the floor?

Then she found she *could* move—without touching the floor. One step, another, another, gliding silently and quickly to the bathroom before she peed herself with fear. In the wetroom she perched on the dripping toilet among the steam while her husband availed himself of the ten separate jets of water that completely cocooned him. He didn't appear to notice that his wife was walking on air; that her feet did not connect with the slippery polished concrete.

The children had to be gathered from the far reaches of the house, where they had their own apartment, almost. She sometimes thought of it like that, their being so far away from the main part with its own high views over the upper reaches of the Manukau Harbour and thundering southern motorway. Barbie's headless body was clutched in Swift's plump hand; in another room Mitch lay with one arm flung over the labrador and his phone clutched tight.

Without touching the floor once she readied them, got breakfast, dealt with a tantrum from Swift who didn't have her own phone yet because she was only three years old. When she handed Mitch his muesli he looked up at her and asked, 'Did you grow in the night?' The dog whimpered beside him. It could tell something was wrong.

She didn't answer, being caught up in the web and the boy in any case going straight back to his phone. A search for *walking above the ground* brought up nothing that could explain. Stuff about Joseph Smith who saw a hovering angel in his bedroom and that's why he started Mormonism. Astral travelling—but you had to be meditating for that, didn't you? And you had to will it to happen. Was this levitation as practised by gurus, spiritualists, charlatans and magicians? But that was also willed—a state that the levitators invited. She had not sought this elevation.

It seemed pointless to put on shoes but there was a strict dress code at work and so she had to.

Out to the SUV where she had to push the seat back for her longer reach. She dropped the dog at doggy care, Swift at daycare and Mitch at before-school care and eventually hauled through the long tail back onto the motorway at Papakura to head north for Newmarket. The last time she had had to apologise for being late her boss had said, 'Get public transport, then, why don't you?' gesturing at her own electric scooter leaning against the wall.

Beg yours? Electric scooters were not public transport and Kimberley's owed its existence to the fact that its owner lived in Parnell, less than 2k from the dental surgery. Kimberley Pemberton BDS was, truth be told, a bit of a bitch.

In and out of the streams of traffic—her old dream again, of being a racing car driver. She could have been, should have been, especially if she'd been this tall. But mostly, stuck fast among thousands of other SUVs surrounding her, she thought of Jack. He hadn't come into the kitchen to say goodbye. She'd caught sight of him through the kitchen window while she was rinsing the kids' cereal bowls. Out on the driveway, head down and engrossed in his phone, he'd only looked up from it when he tossed it on the seat behind him. But it had been like that for years, since before Swift was born, and he was always apologetic: Sorry, hun. Just forgot.

So no point in sending him a hurtie feeling emoji, though she would have liked to. He couldn't help it, even though it made her feel so small it was almost like being invisible.

Into the carpark building, slip into the park next to Kimberley's unused one, up in the lift to the fourth floor above the mall. First to arrive, as she's supposed to be, thank God. Check aircon, wake laptop, coffee machine on. When she got herself a teaspoon she had to bend deeper than usual and caught her hand in the drawer. How long was this going to last? Maybe it would wear off through the day and she'd return to normal. If only there was time to think about it, to find out exactly what it was, but there was a busy day ahead.

At her desk with her coffee Jena had to adjust her chair for comfort, but after that she tried to forget about the gap, getting on with sending out reminders to clients who hadn't paid straight after their appointments, as they were supposed to do. Some of the clients she knew—elderly people living in surprising penury while they clung to their crumbling Remuera piles, or young immigrant families struggling to hold on to their box apartments by the train station. There were kids who'd glugged Coca-Cola from their feeding bottles and been given lollies to keep them quiet, whose baby teeth were rotting out of their heads. People who had reached their thirties and not seen a dentist since they were at primary school. This was the most depressing part of the job, especially the ones whose names and addresses went to the debt collection agency after repeated billing. This morning there was only one of those.

Her finger hovered over the delete button. Could she? Save them from the despair and shame by simply extinguishing their account?

The clip of heels. Kimberley Pemberton BDS.

'Morning.'

A curt nod in her direction. Delete.

'Jena. Anika won't be in today. She's got the flu.'

Anika? For a second the name escaped her. Ah. The new assistant who had started only last week. There had been so many in the last couple of years, unable to put up with KP's snarkiness. Often their flu was a precursor to their leaving entirely.

'I have a procedure mid-morning for which I'll require assistance. Passing instruments mainly, mixing paste for a mould. You've done that before.'

Jena had, on three occasions, when they were between assistants, and it had been an unpleasant experience every time. Kimberley would hiss under her breath or shout, alarming the client but alarming Jena more.

'Irregular but it can't be helped,' said Kimberley, as she had every other time.

At 8am the first client arrived and went through, paid her bill on emerging and disappeared, crossing paths with the second. After he'd gone into the surgery Jena stood up, experimentally. Still pretty much the same, but she'd known that already because her knees were pressing uncomfortably against the underside of the desk.

It was good to be upright. It was good to move around the room, to bend her legs. Probably it was unhealthy for bones not to weight-bear. There was no sense of pressure in any of the joints—ankles, knees and hips swung along as if she were treading water but with less resistance. It wasn't until she went to get another coffee that the uncomfortable truth dawned: she'd grown even taller. Or rather, the gap between the charcoal carpet and the soles of her feet had increased. As she went through the door to the kitchen she fought a desire to lower her head.

Back at reception she found it impossible to fit at her desk. When the client emerged she bent at the waist to process his credit card and he went on his way, unobserving. Why was this happening now, today? What had she done to bring it on? Had she done anything at all? Again she tried to force herself to the floor and again the same soft, determined nudge upwards.

'Please,' she whispered, as if whatever was causing it was listening and might take pity.

The door to the surgery opened and Kimberley emerged, head down over her device, reading client notes. 'The next one's the procedure I mentioned, Jena. Latex allergy. Can you give me a hand to prepare the surgery for ...' She was staring at her. 'What's the matter with you? Stand up straight.'

Very reluctantly Jena did as she was told. Now her hair brushed against the ceiling. Alice in Wonderland. What did she drink? Was it the coffee? Or the wine last night?

'Stop it!' Kimberley's face registered horror. 'I said, stop it!'

'I can't.'

The boss grabbed Jena's feet and tried to pull them down but in the next instant was flung back, violently, as if Jena had kicked her, which she had not. The wounded eyes looking up at her from the floor were at first surprised, then accusatory.

'How dare you?' Kimberley was struggling up, less agile than Jena would have expected from someone who spent most of her free time at the gym. 'I don't know what you're playing at but I suggest you get your things and go.'

'Are you giving me the sack?' Jena's tone was more aggressive than she'd intended. Kimberley, who had previously been two or three centimetres taller, now barely reached her elbow.

'Well, you can't stay here like that.'

'I told you. It's not my fault. It's a ...' She groped for the word. 'Disability.'

Kimberley wasn't really listening. She had taken a long envelope from the desk and was passing it back and forth beneath Jena's feet.

'It's a trick. How are you doing it? This is insane.'

Jena was saved from answering because the next client had arrived, a woman with dark curly hair, which is all Jena had time to register before a sharp scream of terror knifed out of the open mouth.

'Just go, will you? Get out.' Kimberley raced to the client and pulled her close as if to protect her from the monster Jena seemed to have become.

It would be a physical challenge to leave but she grabbed her bag and folded herself into the lift, which was mercifully unoccupied. At full height she moved easily through the ground floor atrium and out into the street, having to hunch only at the glass doors. People were staring and some laughed and clapped, as if she were a busker with extraordinary powers.

What now? Try Jack's number but disconnect before he answers. What would she tell him? That she'd lost her job because Kimberley had taken exception to circumstances that she, Jena, was incapable of altering? He knew what Kimberley was like. Jena had kept him abreast of all the changes in staff; he'd given her advice on how to deal with her vituperative attacks and sarcastic remarks. Stay above it, he'd said. Don't sink to her level. And they'd agreed that female bosses were not necessarily kinder than the male variety.

'Don't rock the boat,' he'd cautioned her. 'We need every cent you earn.'

Their mortgage was over $700,000.

In one stride she crossed the street. Her car would have to stay in the basement garage—she couldn't drive it anyway, now she was around two and a half metres tall. Crowds were gathering on the footpath, traffic stalled at the intersection, everyone staring at her. There were the tiny starbursts of a hundred phones, the high-pitched calls of waving, delighted children, and not too far away down Broadway the blue flash of a patrol car.

Perhaps this—whatever was happening to her—was illegal? From her morning's research she knew it was a rare condition, so rare there were unlikely to be any laws for or against. More likely Kimberley had rung the police and filed an assault complaint. Or the police could merely be concerned that she was causing a traffic snarl.

The safest thing to do, as in many situations, would be to head for home. The safest method to get there would be to walk along the railway lines. If a train came along she could just flatten herself against the sides of the cutting or tunnel. It wasn't as if she were a true giant—she was as thin as ever . Walking was effortless. If she wanted to she could stride the length of the country. She could traverse shallow lakes, leap volcanic cones, side-step rivers.

At Greenlane the railway lines ran beside the motorway and it was discomforting to observe swerving cars and buses slowing and know that she could be the cause of a fatal accident. The distance between her feet and the ground was still increasing. Now her head was above the signal lights and it struck her that it would be in the best interests of the general populace if she were so tall she became scarcely visible, like a jet plane. But the air was thin up there, wasn't it? She could struggle to breathe.

A guard ran out of the station and tried to wrestle her to the ground but he was knocked down, just as Kimberley had been. Several people ran to his aid, some of them uniformed, others concerned members of the public. Two strong men grabbed Jena's feet but the same fate befell them and she strode on, aware of but not sensing the different surfaces below: her air buffered right foot stood above long grass, the left above a swimming pool; the right over the median strip of the motorway, the left on the roof of the Tiptop factory, all the way to Papakura and Swift's daycare. Easy work to pluck her from behind a tree in the fenced yard, where she had been watching a trail of ants cargo biscuit crumbs. If Swift was surprised or frightened it was over in a second. Her delighted arms clasped together around her mother's neck.

Next stop was Karaka Park Primary School, where the children had been let out to eat their lunches. Jena's feet were two metres above their heads so none noticed her, being entirely focused on their lunch and surrounding friends. Mitch, being a solitary boy and given to gazing at the sky when he didn't have his phone, did notice his mother and seemed less than astonished when she lifted him to her hip. Stranger things happened in *Lego Star Wars*. She hadn't carried him like this since he was small and it was an uneasy fit, his strong seven-year-old legs clasped around her waist—but if he weighed on her arms he did not at all on her legs, and she made her way home in a matter of minutes.

Then, as she stood there outside 35A John Key Close, looking down at the crammed silver grey roofs and oblongs of cars and blue rectangles of swimming pools, she began to shrink. Well, not Jena herself, as would be obvious to anyone watching, but the distance she maintained from the ground. Lower and lower and lower still, until she found herself only a few centimetres above the path. Flanked by her children, she walked unimpeded through the front door.

They had lunch on the back deck and then watered the small garden with the hose and Swift's toy watering can. The dry soil around recently planted infant trees soaked up the water as gleefully as the children did her presence. A few times Mitch asked for his phone but accepted, eventually, that she had left it in her car, which is where he would have been reunited with it on a normal day when she picked him up from after-school care. At the kitchen table they drew pictures of flowerbeds, the children creating a fantastical garden with resident horses and elephants and a pear tree with a woman's face. Together they peeled potatoes and marinated chicken for the evening meal. For the first time Mitch wielded the big sharp knife. It was while they were cooking that Jena felt herself return properly to earth with a bump.

All afternoon she resisted the temptation to try to work out what it all had meant. She had walked firmly upon the earth and then she hadn't, and now she did again. She had quite possibly lost her job. Actually, without a doubt she had lost her job.

What had brought on the condition? She tried to cast her mind back to how she had felt when she'd opened her eyes that morning. An odd sense of breathlessness, as if there was not enough air to breathe when there was plenty. Too much, as she'd discovered when she tried to stand up. And before that a sense of panic—impatience for the day to begin and panic that it would be over without a sense of actually having lived it properly; that all day she would be at a remove from reality, rootless, aware only of the pressure to get through it all—the mothering, the hours at work, the mothering again. The chaos in the house.

Deep breath. The right mix of nitrogen, oxygen, argon and carbon dioxide to make her feel like a normal twenty-first-century woman.

At seven o'clock, just as she was finishing the bedtime story, she heard Jack's car in the drive. By the time she had settled the children each in their own quarter and come downstairs he had taken his dinner from the oven and was tucking in, delighted.

'Did you make this?' he asked. He meant 'Surely you bought this?' but at first Jena thought he was asking if someone else in the house had made it. She felt an old-fashioned welling of domestic defensiveness and only just quelled it in time. It was as if she had fallen victim to revisionist, Christian, back-to-the-kitchen anti-feminism. Was it God who had made her lift off the ground? Her parents were irreligious so she had never learned anything biblical from them—but everyone knew about the dowdy kitchen women of Gloriavale.

Or was this state caused by neo-conservatism swooping on women like her, women who tried to do it all?

Or maybe the whole thing had been caused by plain exhaustion.

She poured herself a glass of wine and sat with her husband while he finished his meal. Her bare feet kissed the cool slate tiles of the floor, her knees did not nudge the underside of the table. Mildly they talked of this and that, and she did not tell him she had lost her job. When he asked where her car was, she said she'd dropped it off at the mechanic because it was making a funny noise. When he asked what had happened to the dog, she told him he was having an overnight procedure at the vet. She felt bad lying, but it seemed imperative to keep the peace. She had no energy for argument.

It was only as they proceeded wearily to bed that she registered a peculiar, heavy sensation. As she rinsed her toothbrush under the tap it came on stronger. It felt as though her feet had somehow sunk below the surface of the floor—and yes—her reflection in the bathroom mirror was lower than usual. Glancing down was alarming: it appeared she now had no feet at all. An unseen force dragged at the ten steps she took from wetroom to bedside—not a lot, but still enough to cost her extra effort.

Beside her, Jack skimmed Facebook and checked the headlines before turning his light off a little after ten. Jena lay in the dark, sleepless. What would tomorrow bring? Even if Jack didn't notice that her feet had disappeared, the children certainly would. What if she continued to sink down and down, until only her head was visible skimming above the floor—or worse, what if she vanished entirely?

All over the world women felt themselves losing their grip on their lives or sinking away until they were invisible. She would not be one of them. At midnight she rose, feet dragging, and went out into the garden to find a patch of damp soil that she and the children had watered during the afternoon. The soft earth embraced her, drawing her down until her knees were below the surface, then her groin, then her waist.

A bird landed in her hair, took fright and flew off again. A spider crossed her breast to spin a web at her collarbone. The neighbour's cat sniffed at her trunk, a moth folded its wings against the bark of her cheek. Just after dawn a bee came to land on the blossom of her hand. She knew even less about trees than she did about religion, but the kind of tree she had become was certainly a rapid grower. She could look through the upstairs window at her sweetly sleeping children. She could hope that when Jack woke he would recognise something amiss—his empty bed, the new tree he hadn't planted—and find a shovel to dig her out. He might recognise her as his wife, wash away the dirt from her roots and restore her to human life.

But for now it was all right. It was peaceful. There was no one ordering her about, no one making demands, no pressing chores. She had a place in the earth that was entirely hers and she was standing in it.

LYNLEY EDMEADES

Notice

The kitchen table was warm and beige.
The painter gave us cups of herbal tea
and, as we talked, I folded the teabag label
sideways and sideways again, slowly
revealing a diamond in the desiccating paper.
Two hours passed. Our fathers came into it,
our childhoods, and how they echo.

It's good to see these things, said the painter.
It's our job to take notice. My unborn baby
kept vigil in my growing belly.

What colour is that shadow, the painter asked
as we stepped outside, pointing towards
the dip behind Mt St Bathans.
I was puzzled, word-emptied.
But that's your job, I wanted to say.
You do the names of the colours
and the shadows and I'll do the descriptions.

Like the staunch hush of that mountain.
Like my dry paper diamonds of anxiety.
Like this petrified thrill of taking notice.

STAR GOSSAGE

I have sung my way through this world

1. *Girl with Geraniums in her Hair*, 2019, oil on found ceramic plate, 230mm diameter. Private collection
2. *Flowers from Home*, 2017, oil on board, 800 x 735mm. Private collection
3. *Piki Te Ora*, 2014, oil on board, 850 x 750mm. Private collection
4. *A Day at Pareparea Bay*, 2019, oil on canvas, 455 x 455mm. Chartwell Collection, Auckland Art Gallery Toi o Tāmaki
5. *Kina at the Bay*, 2019, oil on canvas, 455 x 455mm. Private collection
6. *Kahawai at Dawn*, 2017, oil on board, 600 x 650mm. Private collection
7. *Girl of the Dawn Mist*, 2020, oil on linen, 305 x 305mm. Courtesy Tim Melville Gallery
8. *I have sung my way through this world*, 2018, oil on canvas, 1015 x 1015mm. Collection Auckland Art Gallery Toi o Tāmaki

If the pensiveness of the figures in Star Gossage's work emanates a sense of stillness and self-containment, the downward gaze, the closed mouths, the introspective expressions also resonate with melancholy, a sense of taking stock—of the ancestral Māori past, personal loss. These seem like the faces of limbo, of prayer, of listening to karakia out of frame. Even in group portraits, the silence—the figures aren't meeting eyes, nor watching each other—feels potent. The deep inward dream of the face in Girl with Geraniums in her Hair *seems only a semitone away from the solemnity of* Piki Te Ora*; the daubs of paint around the face in* Girl with Geraniums *echo the bouquet of* Flowers from Home.

*Gossage's colour register—of dusk, of a brown earth, of fresh flowers—sometimes makes it seem as if she has dipped her brush in the very substance of the subjects she paints: twilight, chilly dawn sky, beach sand, wet, loose petals harvested after rain. The use of found objects like the plate once used as oil paint palette (or elsewhere, a series of boxes) suggests an expansion of her earlier exploration of links between tangata and whenua, people and their environment. In earlier work Gossage painted with clay. The use of human-made objects as canvas suggests a similar recycling ethos but also a kind of resurrection: the ordinary lifted into intense contemplation; ancestral stories made visible on the detritus of the everyday. —*Emma Neale

Photographed by Kallan MacLeod.

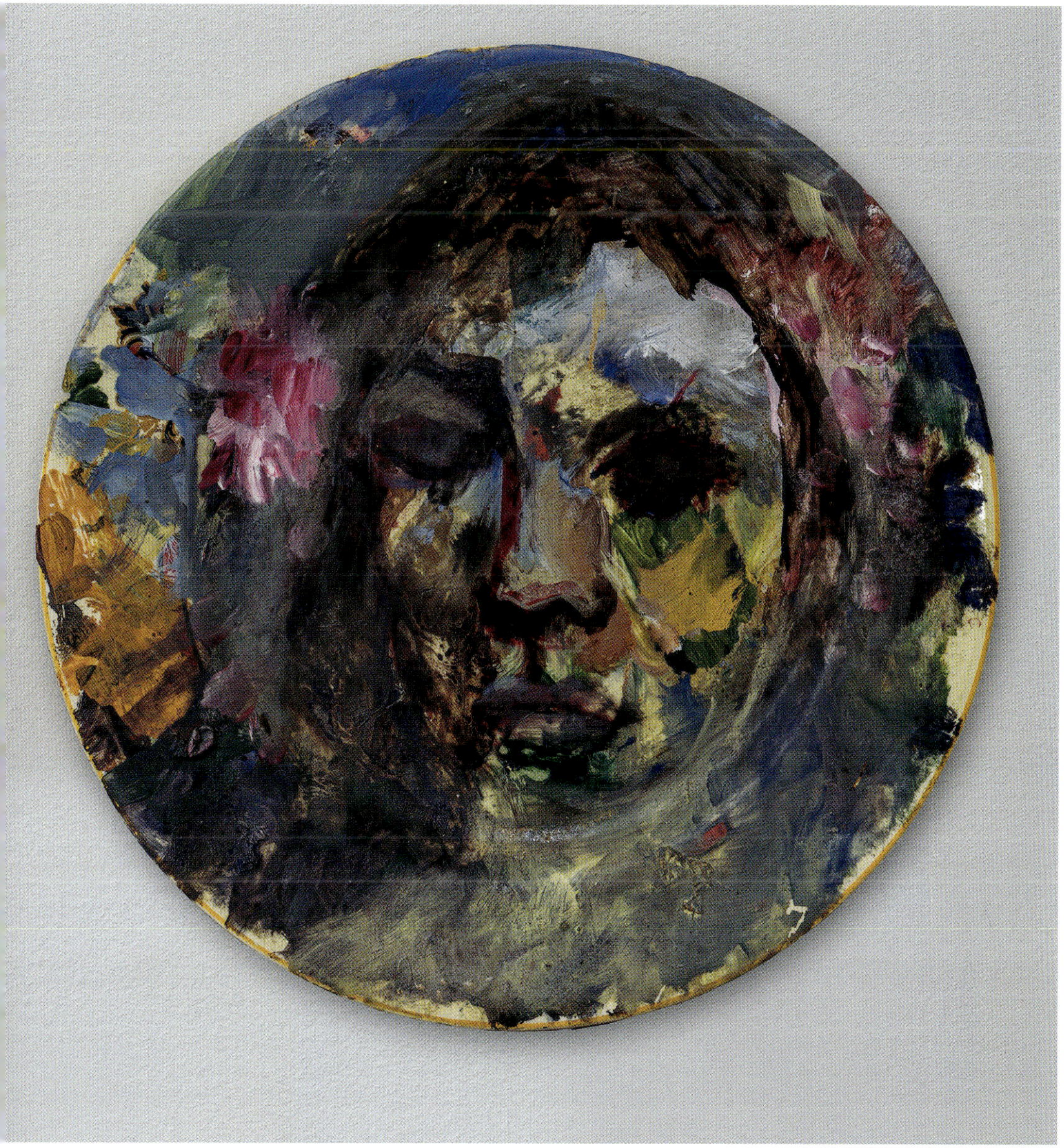

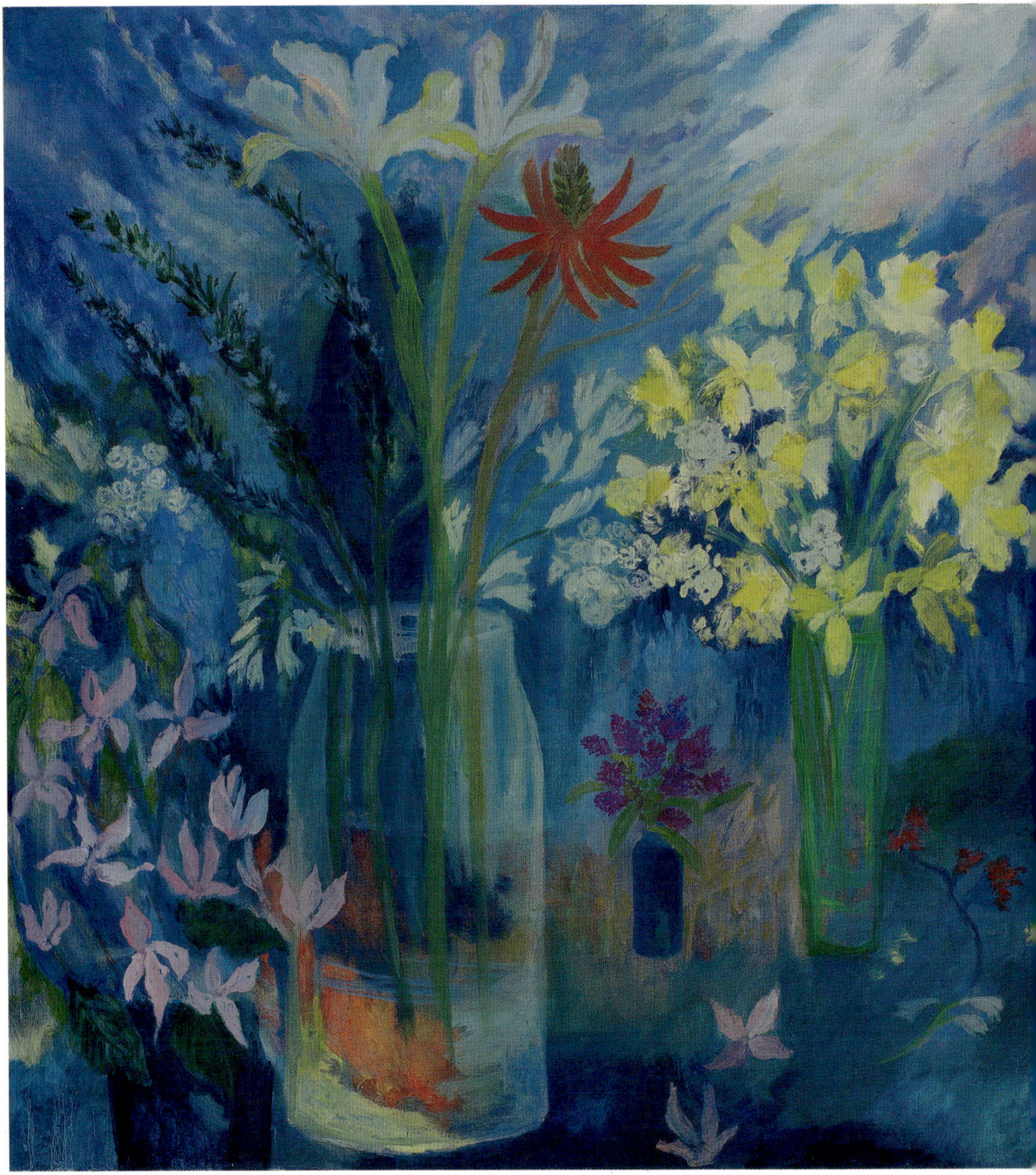

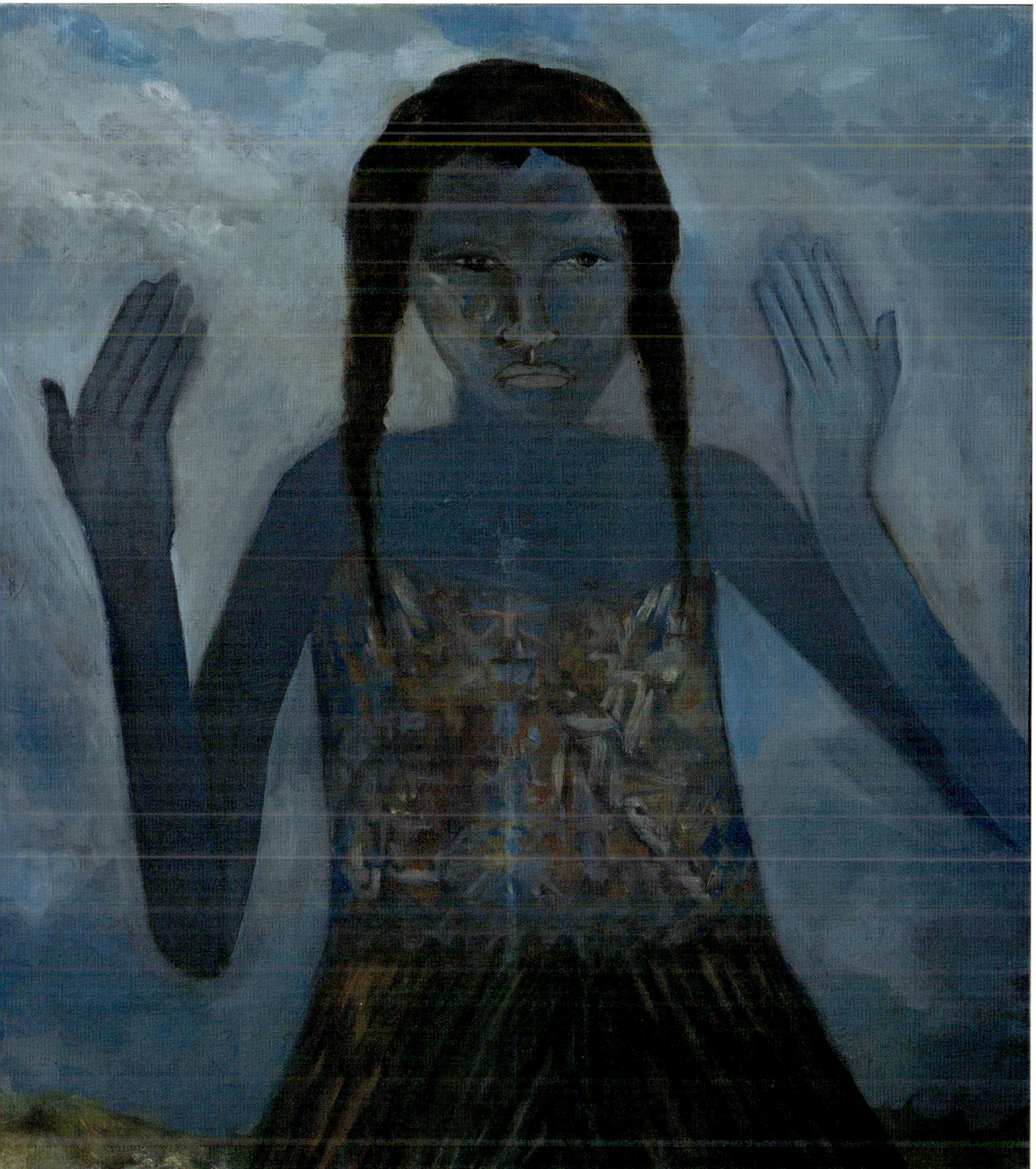

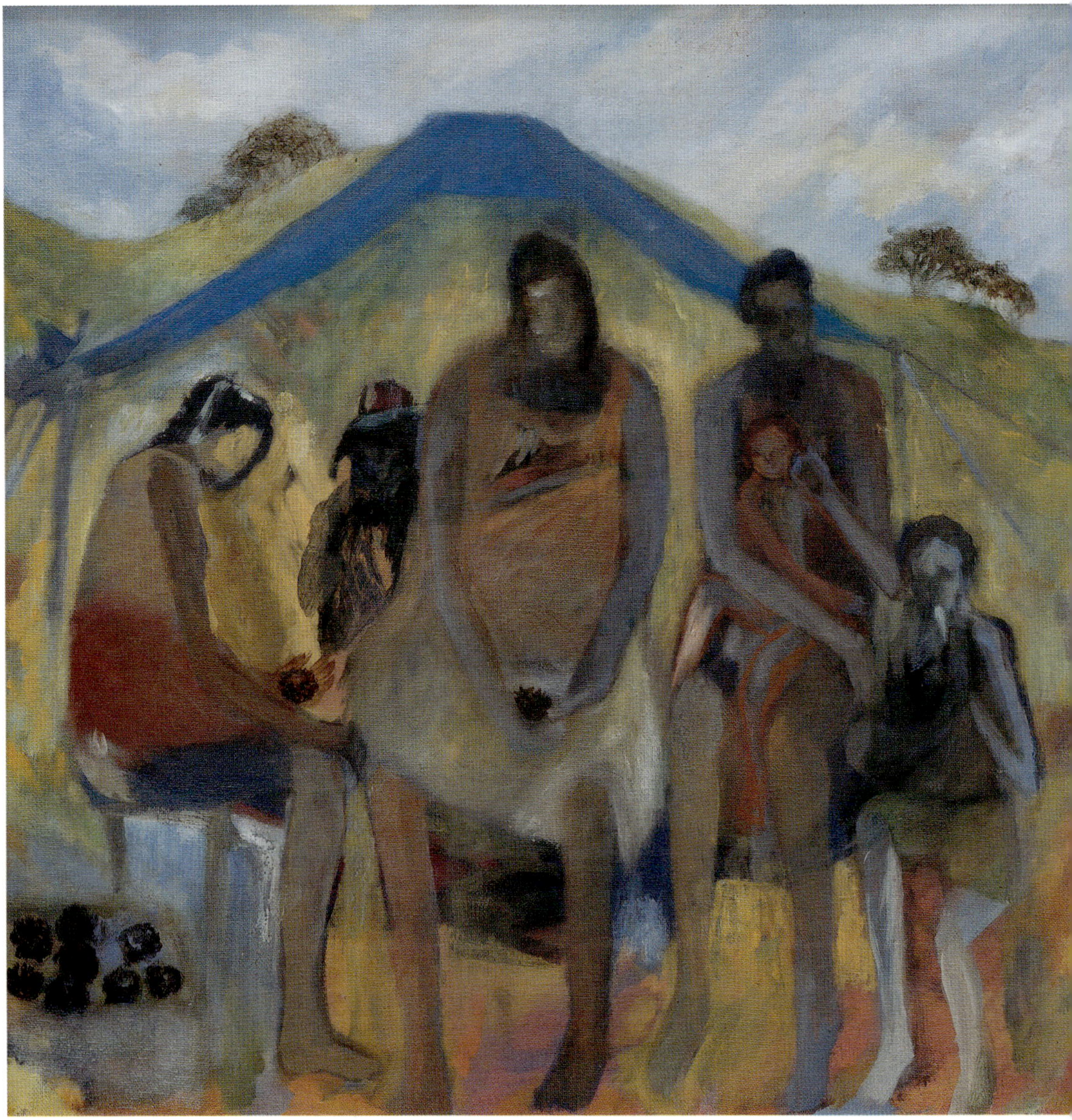

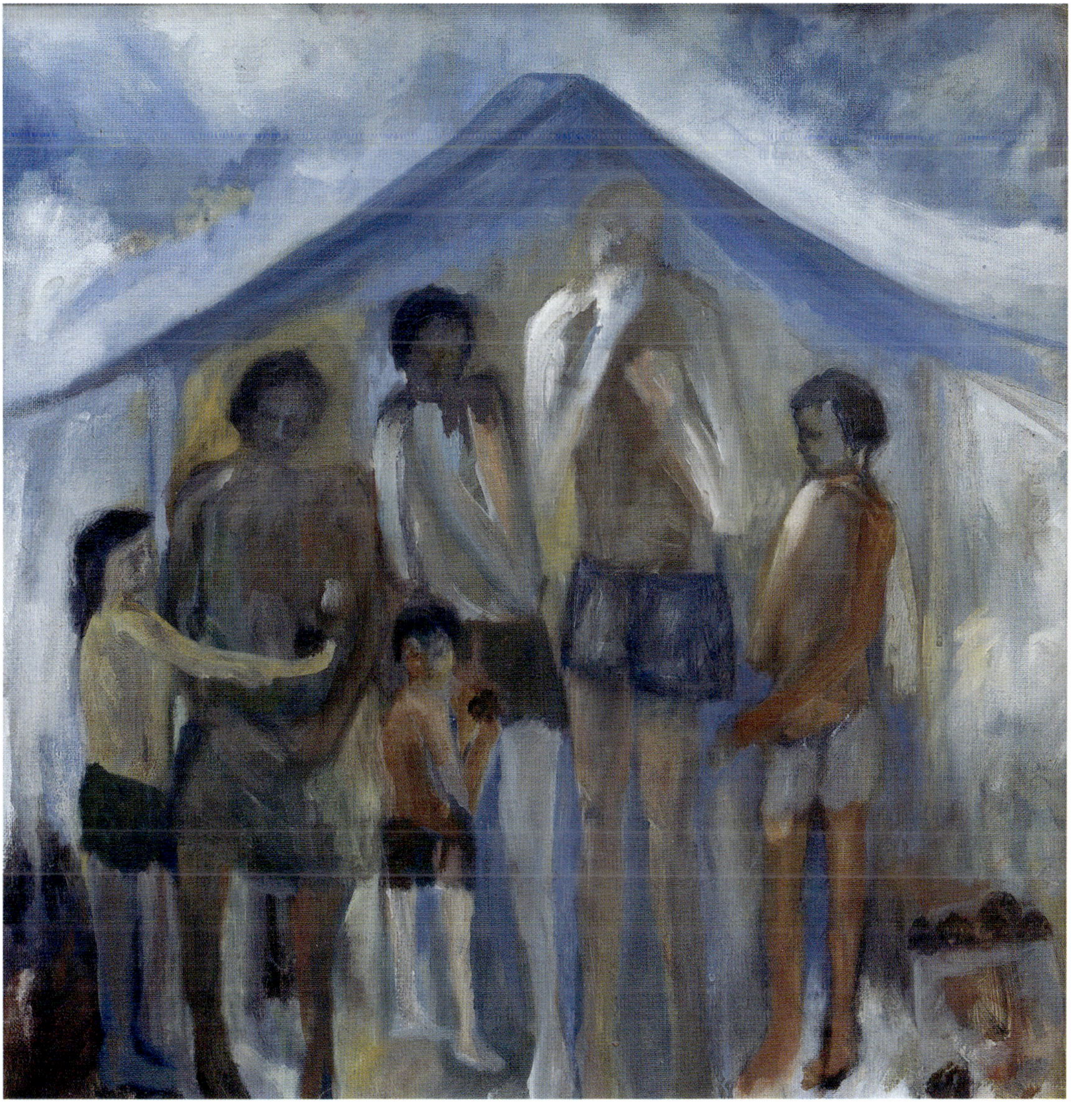

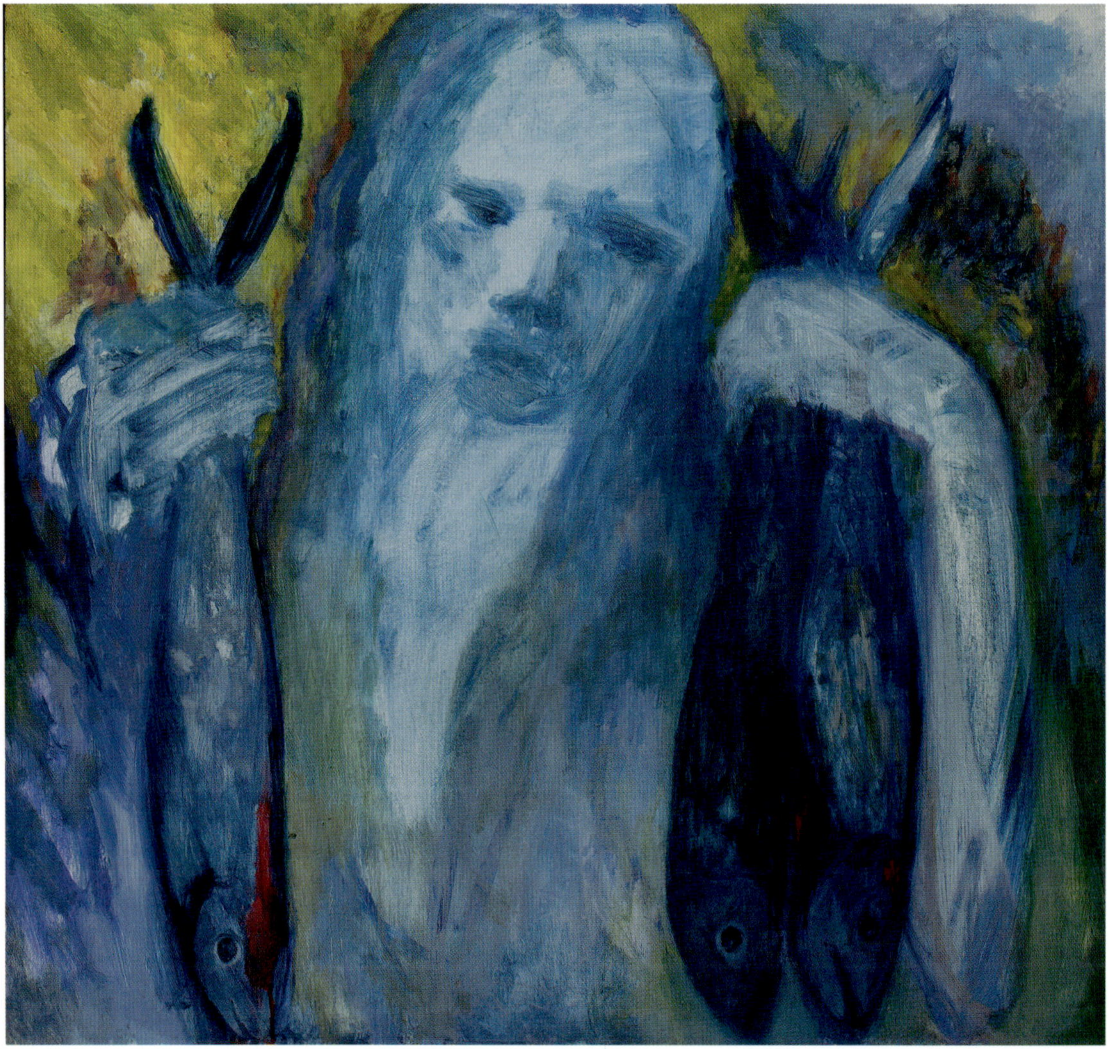

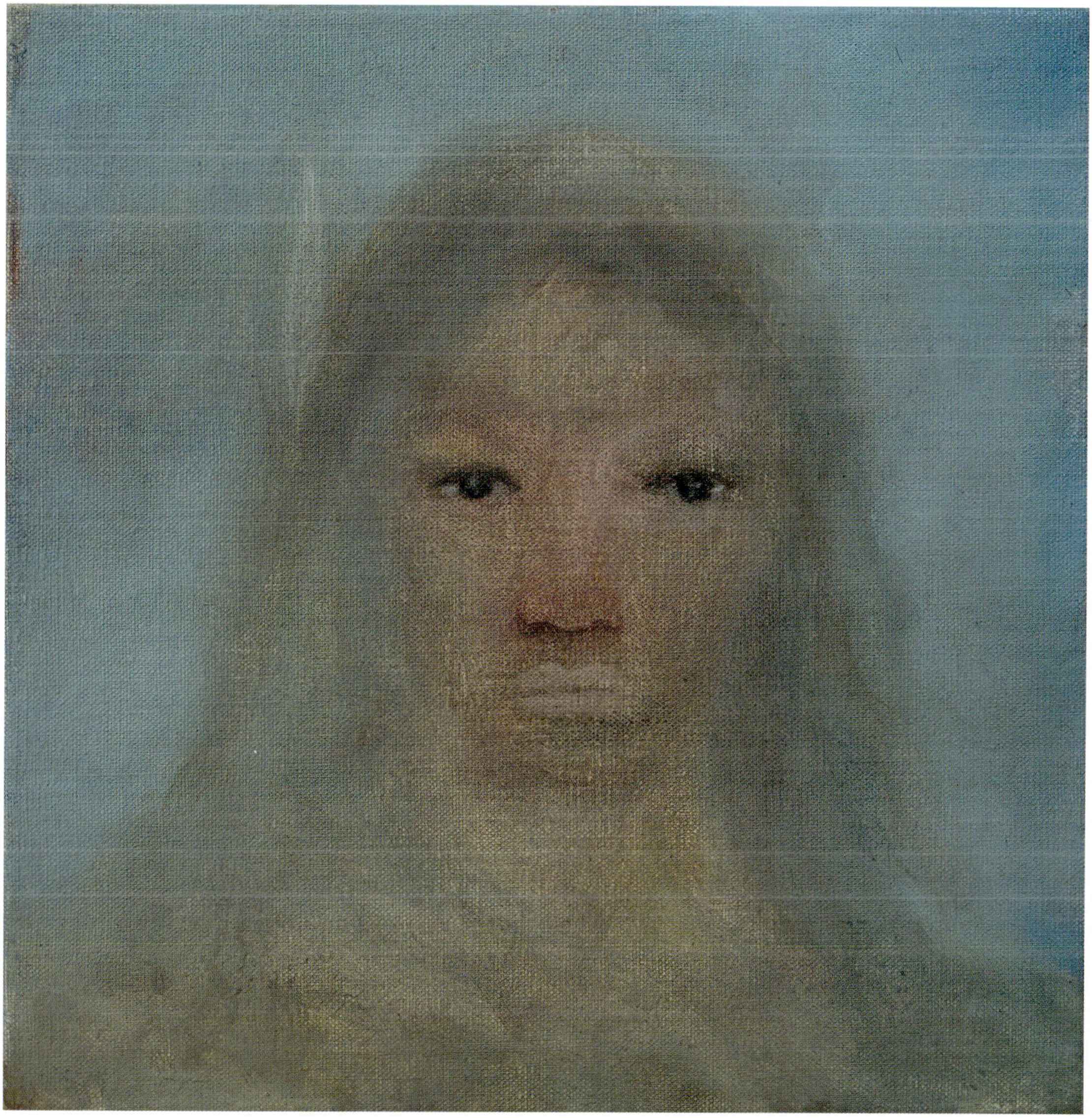

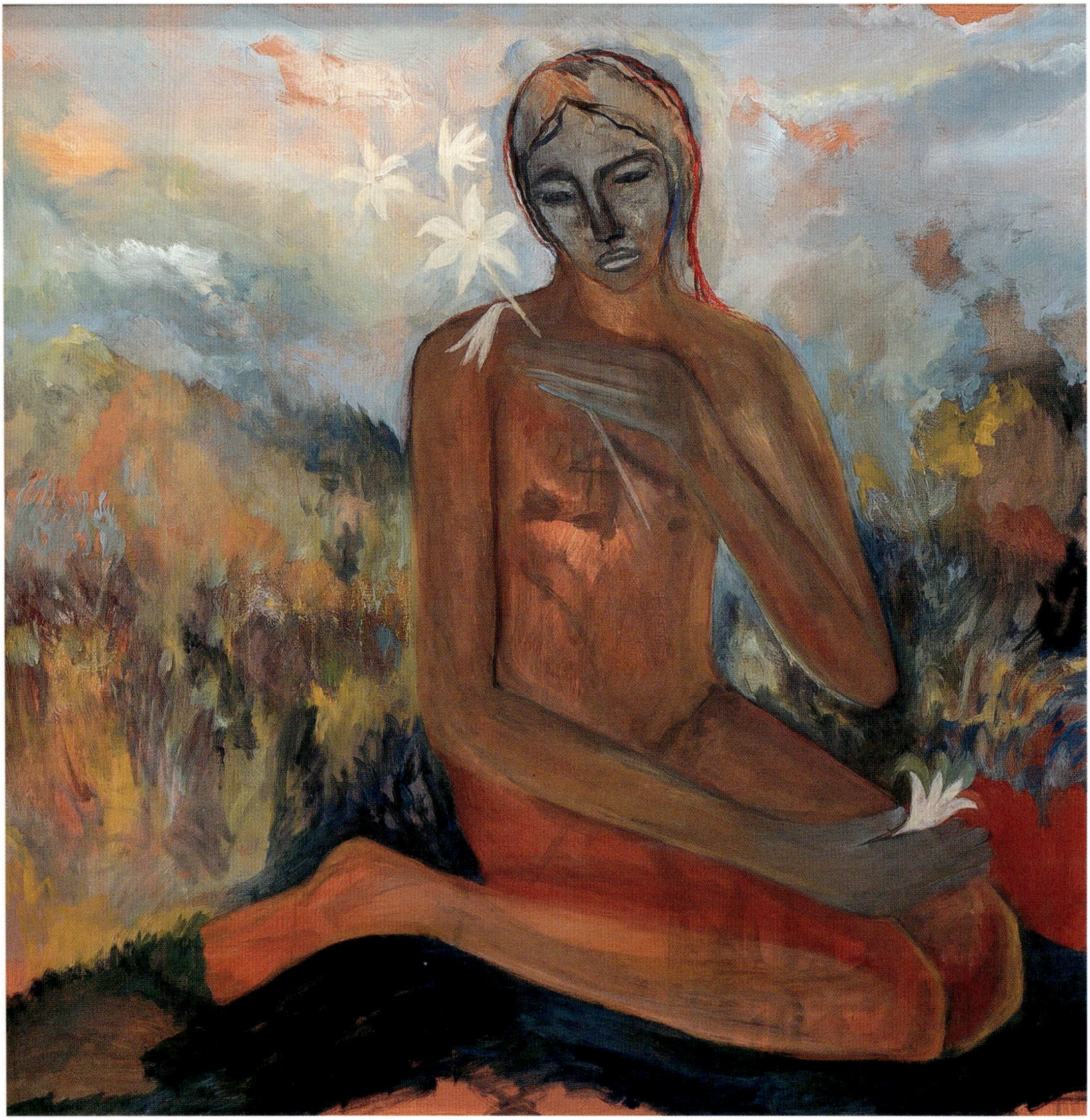

KŌTUKU TITIHUIA NUTTALL

Kēhua

Often, I am looking in the mirror and I do not know the person I am seeing. Some of my features can be explained away to my mother, my aunt, my grandmother—women I have grown up knowing. But the older I get, the more unknown parts of myself I can point to in the mirror. The froglike cheeks and creases on either side of my mouth, certain parts of my eyes.

Sometimes if I look in the mirror at night, I can see the exact image of a woman I do not know. She lives by the ocean and the rainforest. A hundred years ago her people were forbidden to hunt and gather food across all the islands hiding in the Salish Sea. Then they were pushed back to their winter camps, which became reserves. She watched the bounty of salmon, camas, blankets and carvings turn into poverty and violence.

She was stolen away and sent to a residential school. When she returned it was to the deep sickness that had infected her home. The sickness stayed and took her son, my father. The sickness stayed and I wait to fall ill.

BERNADETTE HALL

from 'Fancy Dancing'

xiii.

for my father

She's beautiful in her flowered dress, standing
outside the gate, next to the quiet tree.
There are tiny musical boxes there,
no bigger than thimbles. Domestic, like
her soft attention to her sister,
full of allowances. A little cloudy something
like a plastic button is growing in the left hand
corner of my eye. Humility, ah yes,
it's all about humility. If you were to come back,
I wouldn't rush you. I'd pull the collar
of your coat up around your ears,
I'd lean in on you like a sister, like a mother.
Be careful crossing the street, I'd say,
you've been drinking and I'm worried about you.

TIM SAUNDERS

Demilune

They said the uncle
my father never talked of,
the one who flew sorties
over Germany under a scything moon,
came home only half a man.

I imagined him
split down the middle
like a late windfall apple,
perhaps hollowed out by wasps
or at least limbless,
numb from the waist down
and propelled by a powerful arm.

He went missing
under a moon
that wasn't all there.
They found his clothes
fallen, empty
beside the Ōroua
where the river breaks in two,
palm prints in the wet sand.

ERIK KENNEDY

Online Dream Analysis

Another dream about breaking a tooth,
which means financial loss, or a failure
to be persuasive or courageous, or the death
of a friend or a part of myself,
or miserable or non-existent sex.
They all sound so good, these attacks
from the unconscious on my undefended flank—
my dream-life, which I want to be
full of sailboats and socialism and azaleas.
If I had to interpret the dream, I'd pick the shit sex.
That's reasonably likely to be
someone else's fault, too. I can live with being *half*
guilty of ruining pleasure and having my unconscious spank
me for it. That's the kind of unconscious I can respect.

JENNA HELLER

Fanta Boy

Fanta Boy feels jittery, squirmy, low. So he eats a lime-flavoured sugar disc. Shoves a Fruit Burst in his mouth and takes a few swigs of orange soda. He feels the zing in his veins and the sudden spike settles his nerves as he settles in for another night of gaming in the dark bedroom.

Fanta Boy hears the alarm. Hits snooze twice. Gets up half an hour later. Forgets to check his blood sugar. Injects insulin. Then eats four Weet-Bix with blue milk and three heaped teaspoons of white sugar. Checks Snapchat, showers, dresses. Goes to school, high.

Fanta Boy stumbles from class to class. Visits the bakery for lunch. The best pies in the whole world. Packed with three meats and kūmara with thick, savoury gravy. Buys a Fanta. Downs it all in the time it takes to walk back to school. Endures his final classes then buses home again, high.

Fanta Boy scoops ice cream into a bowl. Chocolate with a chocolate swirl. Packs in half the three-litre tub. Zaps it a little in the microwave. Then hides out in his room for a pre-dinner, first-person shooter binge. Headphones on, mic in place. He talks shit to other boys in other dark rooms eating Skittles, drinking orange fizzy. They're all hoping for pizza tonight.

Fanta Boy kills 89 zombies before dinner. Keeps the game on and checks his blood. High. He injects then devours the lamb chop and pushes the silverbeet and corn around the plate. Twenty minutes later he's back in his room. Chocolate chip cookies in hand. Orange soda bottle propped up against the pillow. Headphones on. Grey graphics spray and flicker across the screen.

His body prepares for an apocalypse.

NICOLA THORSTENSEN

legacy

Dear son,

I'm leaving you
six kōwhai seeds
my recipe for kedgeree
these fragments of the Berlin Wall.

My dictionary
its pressed four-leaf clover
my tortoiseshell comb
your first giggle.

The tang of lemons ripening
the nudge of falling snow
a hug that pays no heed to time.

The cry of a lone albatross
the swell of an aria
the ocean's roar in a tiny shell.

The sorrowful eye of an age-old amphibian
a bear, fur white as surrender
this black-baked earth.

Submerged lands slipped into myth
Venice, Tuvalu, South Dunedin
the terminal face of the last glacier.

JOHN ADAMS

Alexandrine

(for Sasha, aged ten)

If you clench your teeth and sharply suck air, you get it.
Also, on a sandy beach or, better still,
one with pebbles, especially as the water brushes
back to sea. In soft snow, the first run of the day,
blue-skied, cool, skimming the pristine slope,
produces the effect, assuredly, in the shoosh
of solitude. Likewise, that extraction obtained
by wind, inhaling stiffly through shifty groves of olive trees,
wrenched from the agony of leaves, alive,
writhing, oblivious to their lithe circumstances.
The essential Alexandrine sense sweeps
in a broad wave to advance its diminutive form,
emphasising its second syllable, sha. Sha. Sha.
Sa sha, sa sha, sa sha, that's how it sounds,
and, on any given beach, one pebble stands out.

ZOË MEAGER

More River Water

Mother stepped out the back door every morning with a tin jug in hand. 'Mind yourselves a minute,' she'd call over her shoulder. Mother came back every morning with her jugful of river water and emptied it into the porridge pot.

Father appeared at the head of the table and gave us each a wary look: down the row of five on one side, and up the row of four on the other. The two children nearest had their full faces turned to him, and behind them the others were slices of profile: the moon going through her phases.

'Mind me a minute,' Mother said with one hand on the porridge pot handle and the other on her hip. 'I can't be lifting this damn thing alone.' My waxing crescent of a brother leapt up and curled himself to the task.

'More river water, Mother! More river water!'

She gave us ladlefuls. We got twigs in our breakfasts and little critters. Sometimes even a noodley eel.

'It's porridge, you damn savages, so call it porridge.' Her face was red and heavy and the belly of her apron pressed out into the room.

One morning, a duck plopped from the ladle and, with a shake of its head, swam quick circles around my bowl, glinting silvery green.

'Jesus Christ,' Father said. 'How did that get in there?'

Feeling unwelcome, the duck flapped out, spraying porridge all over the sideboard. It nestled into the space on the mantle beside the clock and blinked with each ticking minute.

'There's a lady with no clothes on,' said my new moon of a little sister, so dark behind her fringe she almost was not there.

'There isn't. Where?' said Mother.

'In my river water.'

'Let me see! I want one too!' we all shouted.

'Quiet!' Father said from the end of his long neck. 'Let's see what she's got.'

My sister held up her spoon, and balanced there in a pool of porridge was a woman, slippery as a nymph.

'Steady, mind she doesn't slide off,' said one of my half-faced brothers.

Mother ran a quick tongue around her top teeth and plucked the woman up by her hair, dangling her for inspection.

'Wak! Wak!' said the duck, swooping down from the mantle, its body an arrow pointing at the tiny bread-coloured woman. 'Wak!'

Mother swung the woman into her waiting mouth and with a pop, drew her out again, clean as a cockabully.

ELIANA GRAY & JORDAN HAMEL

Down the old quarry, water feels like velvet

It's a concentration of minerals
slide them over my skin
there's no movement in a quarry
lake no river to run only the
push of our bodies through the
mineral water to breathe in the
mineral air

The water is dense with ghosts
maybe that's the reason it feels like
velvet maybe when the lake was made
some didn't make it out the high sides
of the pit closing in water rushing to
support that carved out rock sluiced for
gold maybe that's what we're feeling the
ghost of a movement

Up and up in hydraulic fashion
swimmers bob with chemical
buoyancy do they know about the
kilaire el dorado drips downhill
water crusts mid-alchemy a
sediment silt fog

The streets are coated in it
gorse wrestles empty stores
for control a population fleeing
not ready to swim not ready to
drown wagons hitched to
somewhere with less opportunity

Everything begins to feel thick
accumulated at the bottom of
a lake a place a reiteration of
itself clustering around ankles
the corners of our mouths it
flakes off lips and gathers

Unsettled specks in constellation
hand drawn shores pulled tight
sucked in pressure flattening
particles exhaled ore we extracted
everything compressed into spectre

Information is never really lost
yes we are transferable in matter
yes but what are ghosts if not an
imprint a transformation of water mid
alchemy a concentration of minerals
a density of silt a liquid that pushes
back reminds you that it's there
it coats your skin it feels like velvet

ISABEL HAARHAUS

Rat

Rat was very good at drawing. Genius even. It made sense I suppose, given his intensity and keen aesthetic. But it did come as a surprise when he showed me the ballpoint drawings. It was as if he had shoved his fist down the throat of some animal, rubbed his knuckles along the wet oesophagus and then drawn what he felt; as if he had squeezed in his hands the body of a bird or a cat so tight that it broke, knowing each tiny bone, how it fitted with another, and then sketched the intricate pattern. The detail was astonishing, as was the trace of concentration: tightly complex spidery lines testament to somebody bent over paper for what must have been hours, days, even weeks some of them. There were no beginnings or endings in Rat's drawings—bodies and shapes morphed together, interconnected and endless.

Rat was one of the ones who didn't make it, and that was no surprise—not when you thought about what I heard the one night I stayed with him at his mum's house. Just straight-out abuse, just a constant stream of it, and for no apparent reason. What was so weird about that night was how unfazed Rat was. He took it as if it was just a bit of drizzle, not the outright thrashing storm it was. Thinking back, he would have been only about fourteen or fifteen then, though he did his best to look older. He was just a kid, but by then already all black leather and buckled boots, and matted hair and hooded eyes. There was always something about him though, and that was what came through in those pictures. They were shocking, entrancing, beautiful.

There were a lot of Goths around at that time. At school there were heaps and they were always killing themselves. One after another all through fifth form. They kept ferrets for pets and stayed out of the sun and seemed to hate everyone, most of all themselves. And then they topped themselves.

But Rat was more than just a Goth, he was like a Punk-Goth, or a Gothy-Punk. He certainly had a sense of humour. He must have been really intelligent, actually, when I think of it now—he was strangely self-aware, often reflecting on what we were up to in a slightly bemused, ironic way.

'Ah yeah,' he might drawl as we hurtled over the harbour bridge in Jonny's Mini, 'Scraping Foetus off the Wheel' screaming on the tape deck. 'Ah yeah, this has got to be the part where I put my arm like this and try to poke you.' Or, 'Mmmm, this is surely where we crash and burn.' He said that often, with a creepy self-satisfied smile in his voice: malice mixed with pleasure. It was like he was behind the camera looking at his own life, but unable or unwilling to properly direct it, sort of like the reality TV shows that would later become ubiquitous, where no one is allowed to intervene, only watch the contestants tear each other to shreds and slowly but surely hang themselves.

On Saturday nights we always went to the Bermuda Flats in Avondale. It was just the place to go, and when we got there Rat would give Melanie's mum a footbath. He must have been in the habit for ages, certainly since before I knew them, because no one much commented on their little ritual. Rat was almost a bit camp when he did it, like a caricature of a small-town barber. He'd say in a dodgy Cockney accent, 'Come on, then, Mrs Mel, come and sit by the fire and have a soak.' Not that there was a fire, just a couple of sparking electric bars by a hole in the wall. The carpet was sticky and the one table low and wet. But it was like something out of Coronation Street the way those two carried on: banal and neighbourly and strangely cosy, somehow entirely removed in their little corner by the curved wall from the drug-taking and random bursts of violence going on around them in the small crowded lounge.

Melanie's mum would play her part, smiling indulgently at Rat's flourishes, her stretched veined cheeks dimpling, her eyes squinting and wet. And she would allow herself to be seated by that electric heater in front of the blocked-up fireplace in that stony little room, clutching onto Rat's leather-padded shoulder as he lowered her down onto the sagging yellowish couch, and let the boy arrange and tend to her big swollen feet in the orange laundry bucket.

She was a prison guard and her feet were purple and thick with fluid on top, and dry-cracked and white around the edges. She was on her feet for twelve to fourteen hours a day and the only one with a proper paid job in that house. It was hard to tell how old she was but she looked old to us. She was exhausted and a steady alcoholic. She'd sit there, her feet in the lukewarm water, sipping her white cask wine from a brown coffee mug, and just vaguely observe from her fuzzy distance what went on, shaking her merry little head, tut-tutting, and occasionally cackling with laughter.

Everyone loved Mrs Mel, even though we never knew her actual name. She was Melanie's mum and Rat was her favourite.

When Rat stayed at my place he wasn't quite so chivalrous. We were teenagers and the boys were just always trying to get the girls into bed. It didn't even seem to be so much about the actual sex, which was mostly just embarrassing, or funny at best, but about the conquest and the notching and bragging afterwards.

'Didn't you fuck her?' you'd hear them goad each other. 'What are ya, a fuckin' homo?'

Rat was really tall and skinny and pretty filthy. That was all part of the look, I guess. His pants were so tight that he mostly couldn't get them off by the time we got to bed anyway, because by then we were all so wasted. He wore the biggest, chunkiest boots, which caused his skinny body to sway over them, like a Len Lye wind sculpture—you could imagine him making that metal twanking sound, the sound of thin long strips of metal bent by the wind. That was Rat: bent by the wind and looking like he was about to topple over at any time.

He never exactly forced the girls, but he was pushy. He'd fix on you for the night and sort of flatter and humiliate you at the same time.

'You look all right tonight,' he'd say, looking you up and down, smirking. 'I like a girl in ripped tights. So original.' It was hard to know if he meant it or was mocking you. Worse still, he'd completely ignore you. He'd try to poke you one weekend and then completely ignore you the next. It was one of the many things in that scene, at that time, that left you feeling bewildered, not knowing where you stood with him (or anyone else, for that matter), how to react, how to take it. Not knowing whether to laugh or push him away when he did finally come on to you or just to tell him to fuck off from the start. And sometimes if he felt like he wasn't going to get anywhere with you that night he could just really turn on you. He could be scathing, shouting to the others 'Why is this stupid little slut coming with us?' and, worried you might not get to go along to wherever they were all going, you'd spend the rest of the night trying to get his attention back, trying to win his approval.

It was weird because his power came from the fact that he had nothing to offer in the end. He was Rat and he had nothing except those stupid oversized boots he wore, covered in chains and padlocked. He had nothing to offer and even less to lose, which turned out to be quite a powerful position to be in, for a while anyway.

When I saw him around years later he was a full-blown junkie and didn't recognise me, or pretended not to. He had a son and the rumour was that one night he and his girlfriend were cooking up and spilt the acid they used in the child's eyes and now the boy is blind.

Rat died in Christchurch. He would have been only about twenty-two or three, but by then he was known to half of Auckland and most of Christchurch. People felt passionate about Rat: they either hated him or loved him. I loved him in a way.

I loved the way he tenderly lowered Mrs Mel's swollen feet into that scuzzy footbath and flirted with the old drunk woman. I loved all the cruel ways he made me feel alive to every outline, every word, intonation and gesture on those crazy Saturday nights at the Bermuda Flats. Where you sat and how you sat there. Who you sat next to. What you said and how you said it. Somehow Rat held court there and it was his approval we all sought as we arranged and rearranged ourselves in that little wet room. And I loved the drawings that he showed me one night after he'd failed to get me into bed: drawings of wild, raging, intertwined creatures; tortured, intricately detailed and cross-sectioned creatures; creatures that showed you what the inside of a cat might look like, how a long throat works, how a rodent's skeleton is made to flatten itself into the narrowest of spaces; creatures that showed you what it was like to be a boy who went by the name of Rat.

SARAH SCOTT

Chrysanthemums

She lies dusking in the catkin dust.
He looks up from his sketchbook.

He's a bit worn out and the warm grass grazes him.
He places a sketch on the anted ground

that smells like the little plain plants heating up.
She tells him *they're called chrysanthemums,*

they're a place for moths to be born
the colour of beerhead and seafoam

flocking. They quicken to the bud.
She colours in his eyes the colour

of the worn sea that crazes him.
She draws dusky wings above her

worn way back on her back like plain plants.
The way a bud is a flock locked up.

MEGAN KITCHING

A Bee Against a Window

A bee against a window
crawls, sidles, then drops
dogged, like a swimmer
under a waterfall, pummelled
by the pipe-organ drone
of its own labours. The glass
viscous as summer air
ripples with grains of light.
Flowers stain those waves
and the bee quivers, tasting
(not quite yet) their sweet sonar,
and shoulders steadily on.
The blunt head nudging
for a change of pressure,
a crack where its song
will mute, a swallowed echo,
and rush through into streams
beyond. The bee knows no sides
only sunwards until
it tires, rests in the hammock
of a corner. It cannot lie
like glass or twist colours
like distance or sly through
that other, open window.
But climbs steadily on.
One instant lofted free
and the bee will forget
with what patience it now
gnaws towards a day

upon the rim of summer.
Between is this wing, this waxen
slice of sky, this slipping wall
the bee scales, forever.

GILLIAN ROACH

Barbara Eden's Screams

1.
It was the 70s.
There wasn't much on.

They lured us in
with cartoon credits

smacked us
with the laugh track.

Why weren't we laughing?
Why were they?

2.
Jeannie's bottle—
patriarchal symbol but damn
inside it looked cosy.

3.
Also, weirdly, erotic.

4.
So many situations
dissolving via pink smoke
into a mulberry cushioned
safe space appeals.

5.
Although …
bathroom, bedroom, kitchen?
Not much real
estate in that thing.

6.
Where in a world curved
in on itself
does the fetching light
on your boobs
originate?

7.
'Despite the fact Jeannie is subservient to Tony Nelson, she is still ultimately an independent and capable woman.'
—Barbara Eden

8.
<<cough>> Stockholm syndrome.

9.
Honest opinion?
Way more fun to be a genie than have a genie.
Fucking annoying, some sarcastic broad
hanging off your neck causing chaos.

10.
No agency? Come on,
that bottle waggled about
like no one's business,
drawing cute attention to itself.

11.
Anyone surprised Hagman was a jerk?
Clearly not the star. Well down the list
behind the bottle, Barbara
and those diaphanous pants.

12.
Poor Larry, angry alcoholic
man-baby who urinated on set
and abused guest actors.
Well, enough about him.
Once the director left Barbara Eden
trapped in a prop bottle for two hours
while the cast went for lunch.

13.
Pizza, pasta, burger—
what could you stomach
knowing you've left a woman
in a bottle?

14.
(they taped her screams and used them in the show)

15.
We weren't laughing,
I like to think we sensed it.
Something mean.
The echo of Barbara Eden's screams.

SUSAN WARDELL

High Country Hallelujah

He tells tales of a high-country faith
at the mercy of snow on loose rocks
their fellowships of Sunday roasts
with unwashed shearers—salt kind of folk
and they had to be the light.

On holy days they prayed alone, but I wonder
if she washed the socks of visiting prophets?
Sheared minutes from her household schedule,
hem-swinging children, in prayer
for wool prices to allow a new oven.

Sometimes I've seen her—
in the kitchen her mother paid for—
crawl into the thousand-year thicket
of her William Morris mug, and wait
as pomegranates split open like scalded pink knuckles

while over her flocked shoulder, and out the window,
their strange, quiet son is gorging himself
on crabapples, snake green and hard as sin
and all the while knowing
that doubt has room enough for them all, within.

God took apart the mountain, and the man.
They moved to town. Twenty years on
their faith is anything but suburban.
It wakes itself early. *God is preparing us*
for greater things.

The children have gone.
So on weekdays she tends the sick
in her winged sneakers, and on Sundays
she watches his square brown fingers slow-tug
at the bass guitar. Made sound.

The service stitches their weeks in a row
but at night she practises 'crazy quilting',
lets vines roam over linen edges and lines.
Sees how, through that small silver point,
everything shines.

VITA COCHRAN

This Elaboration

Eight panels, 2019–20, New Zealand wool on Belgian linen, 235 x 155mm

When someone embroiders the truth, we mean that they are falsely enhancing what really happened. When we say that they are embroidering a story, there's a similar sense that the true core of things is being added to in a frivolous or fanciful way. By why shouldn't embroidering be the whole story? Why shouldn't it be the plot you follow? The metaphor 'to embroider' should mean, I think, something more like tell, or extend, or pursue or discover. Thoughts like these are how I came to this, this elaboration: a story in stitch, colour and geometry. — Vita Cochran

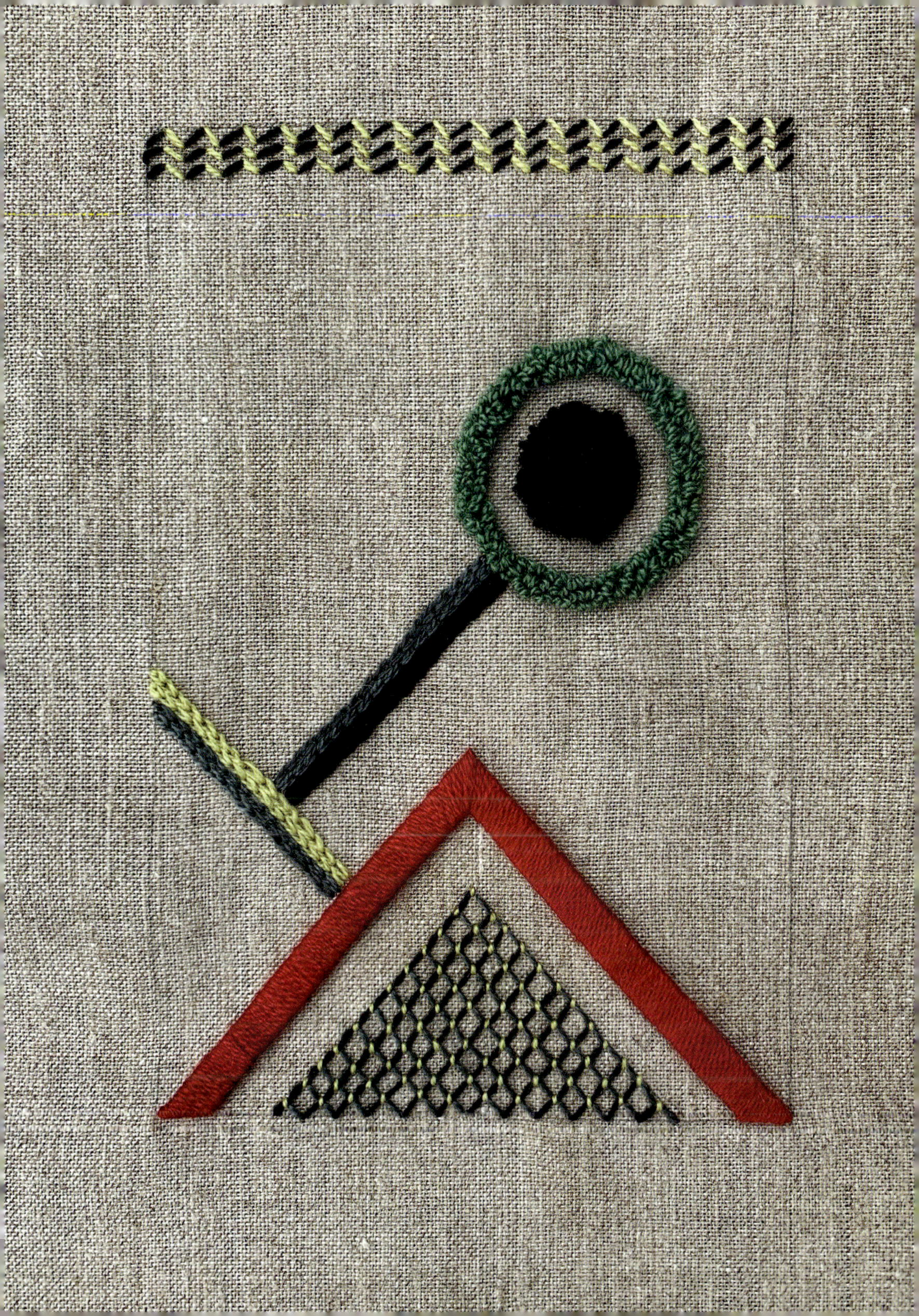

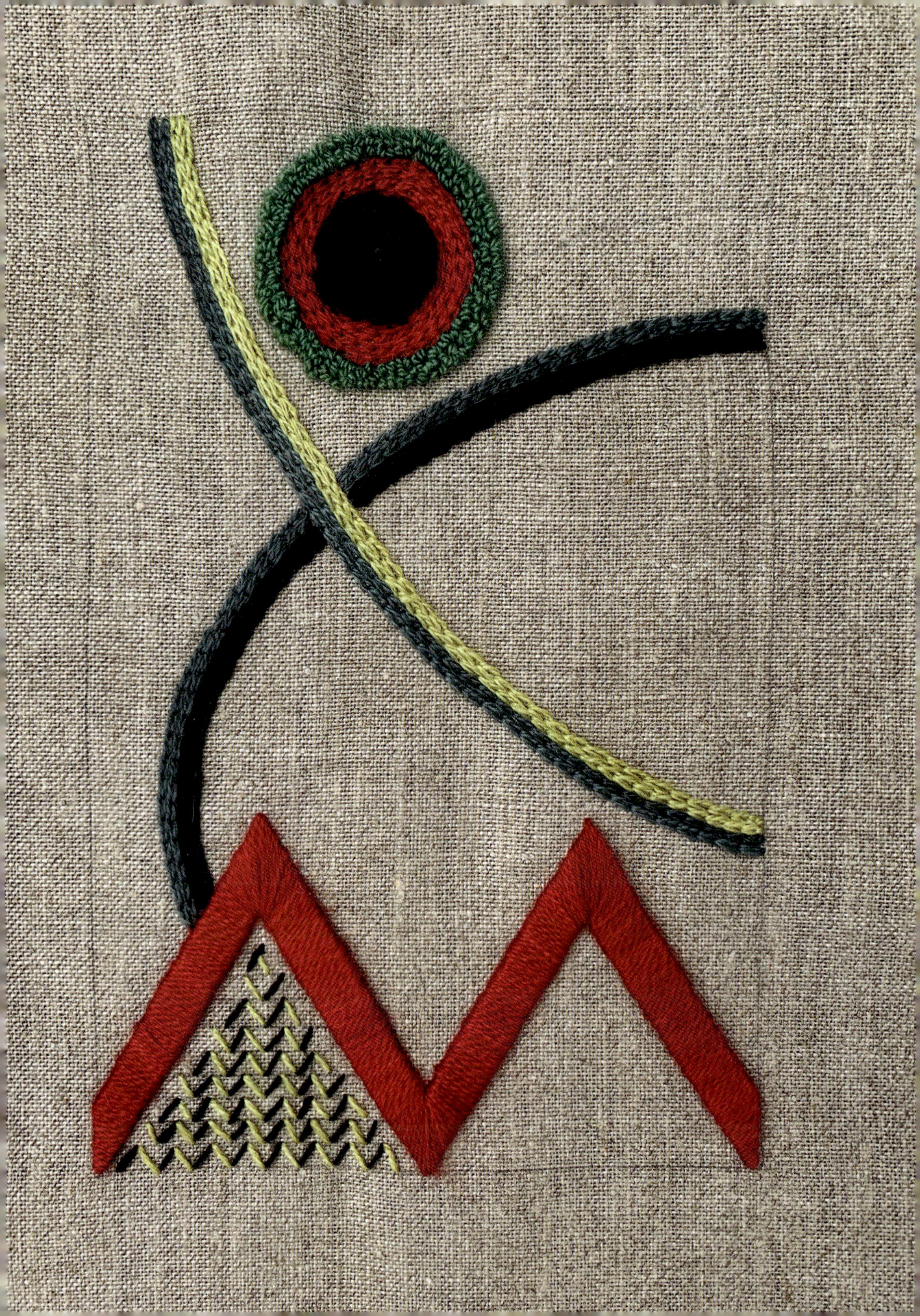

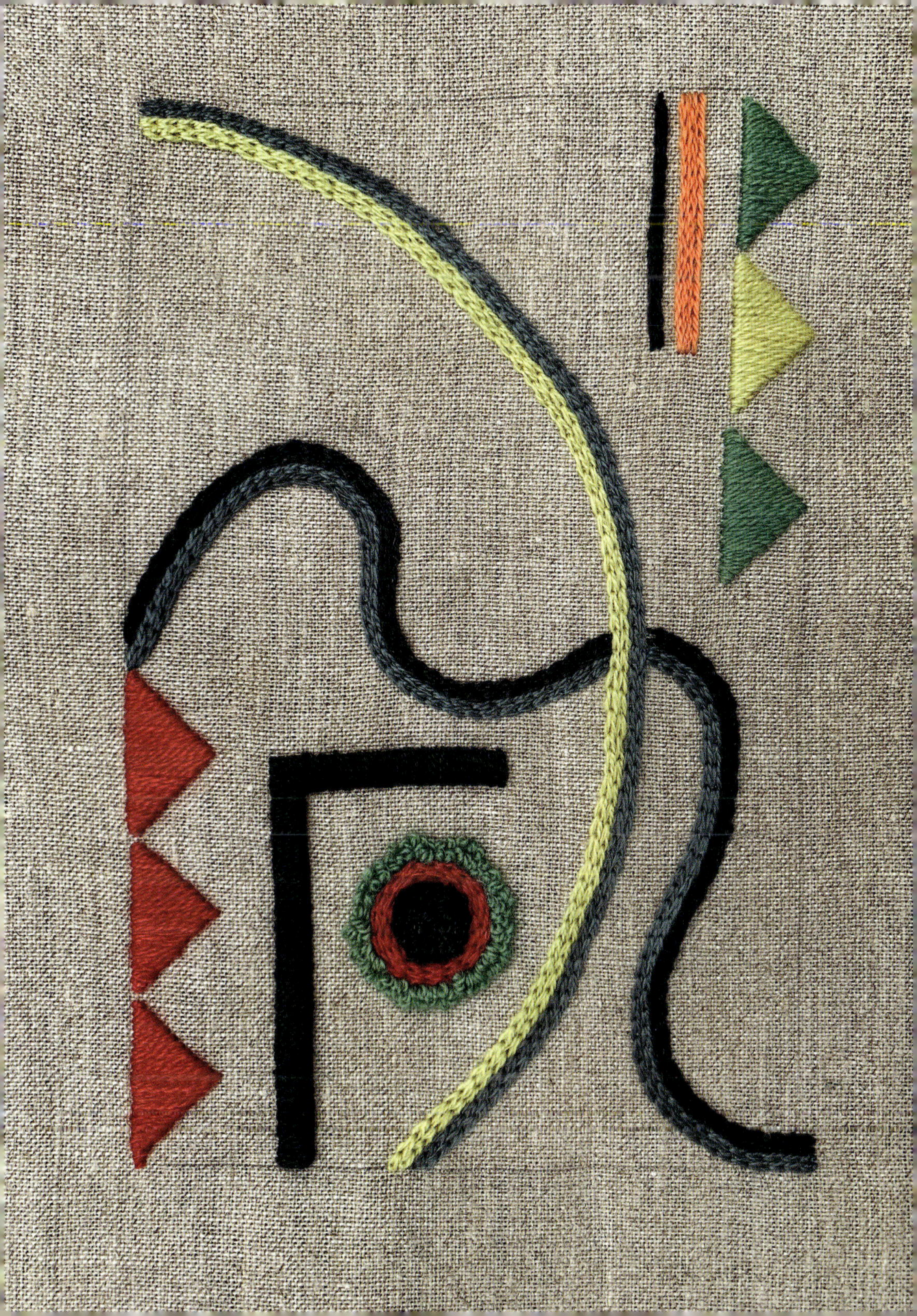

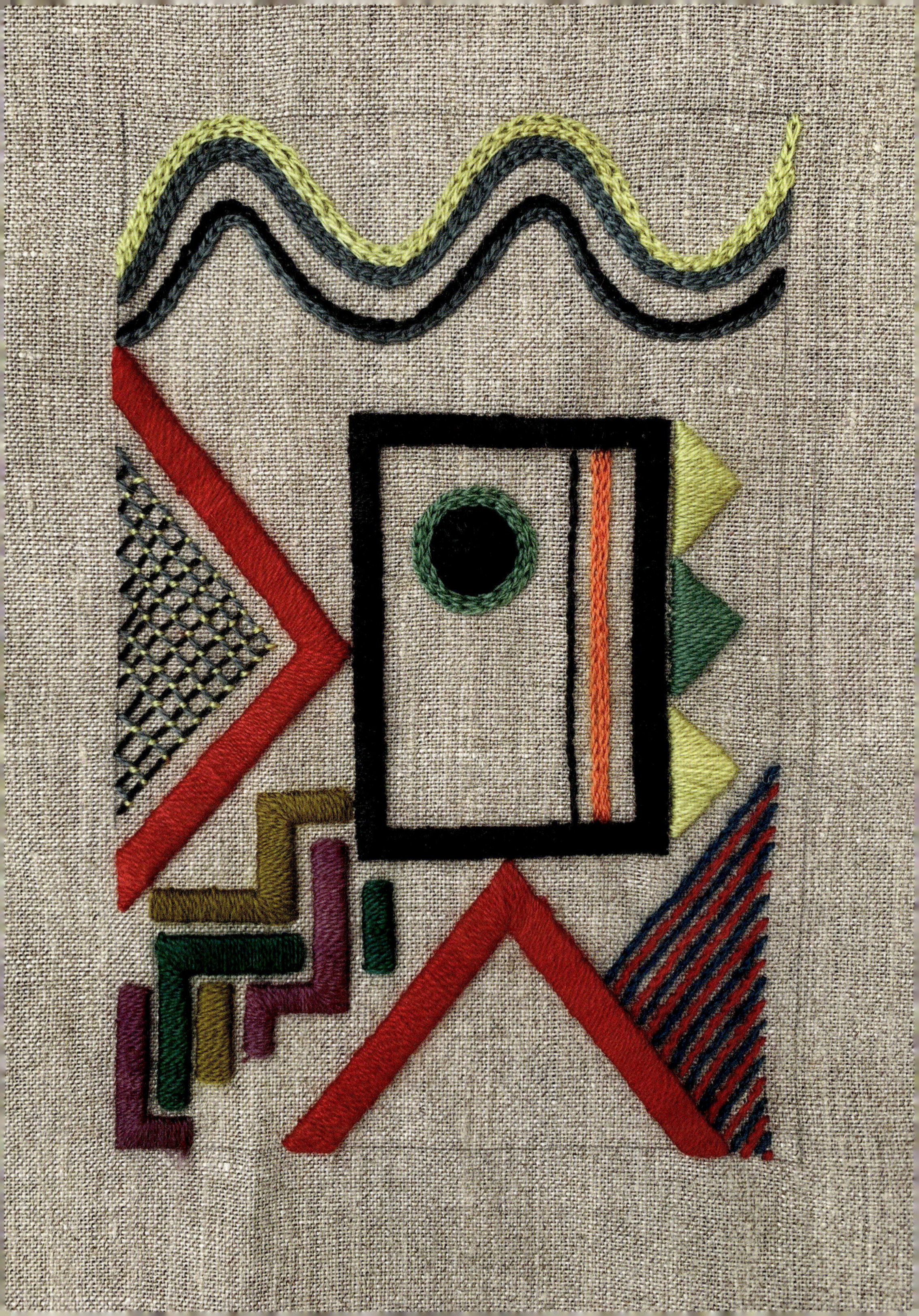

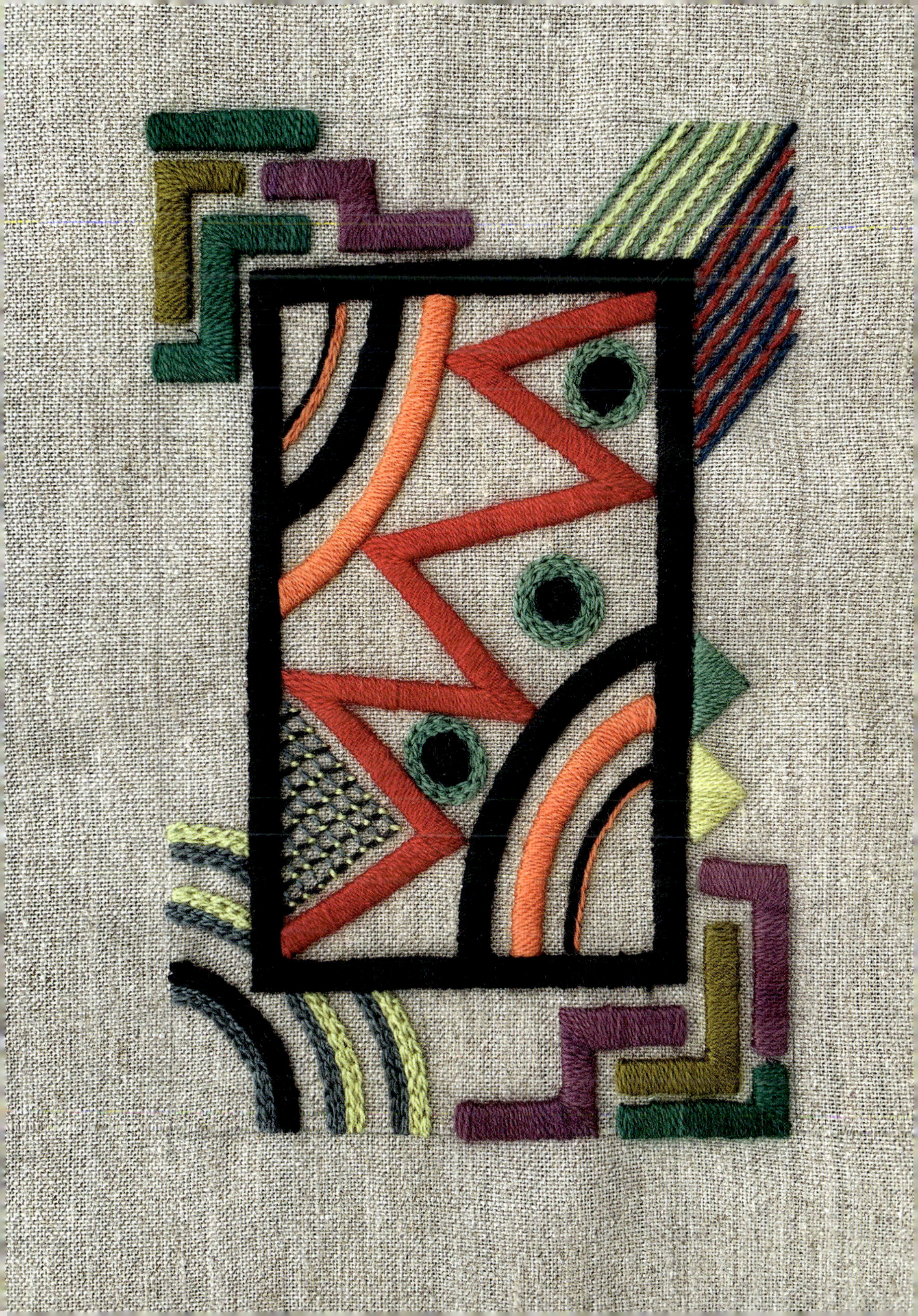

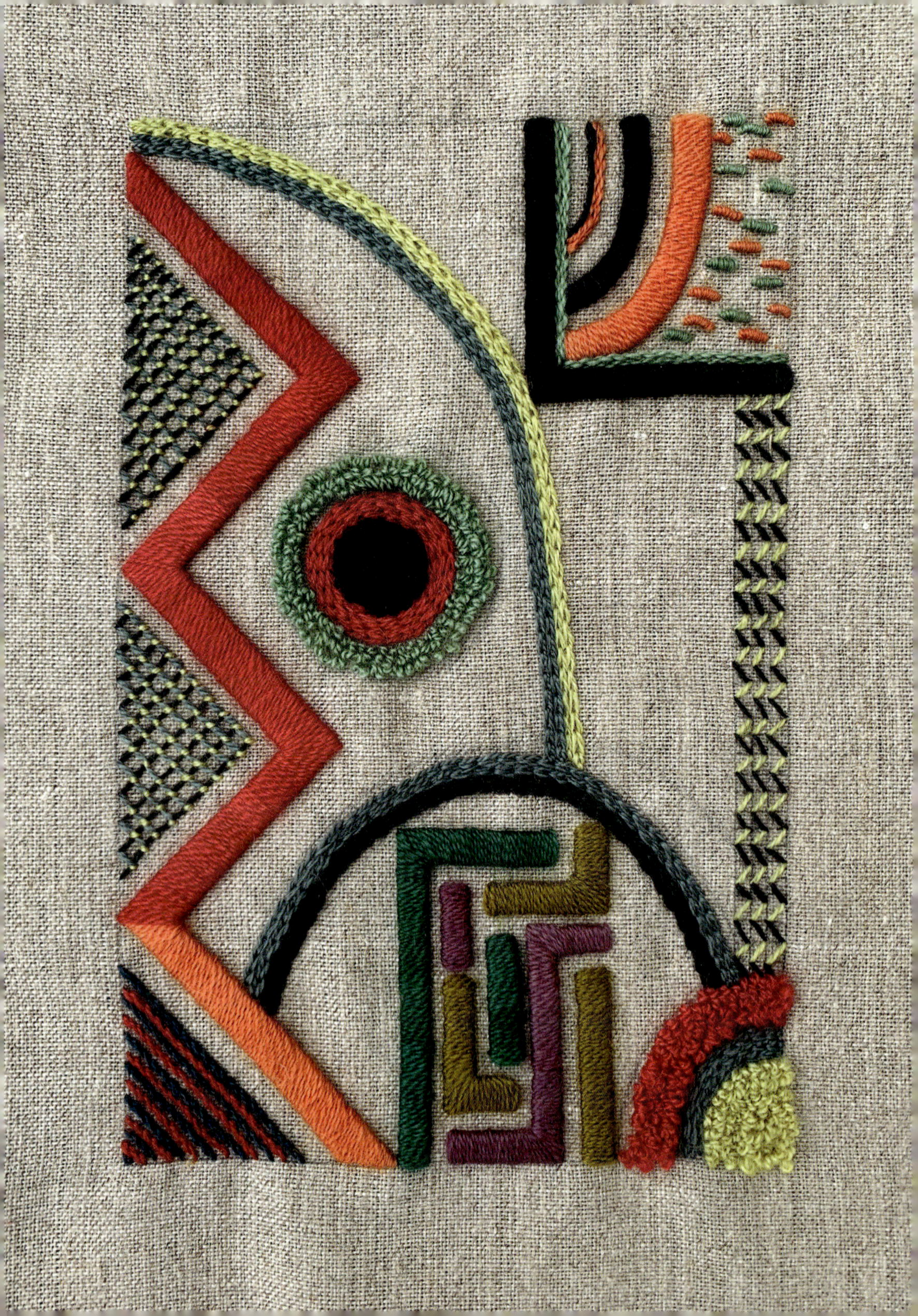

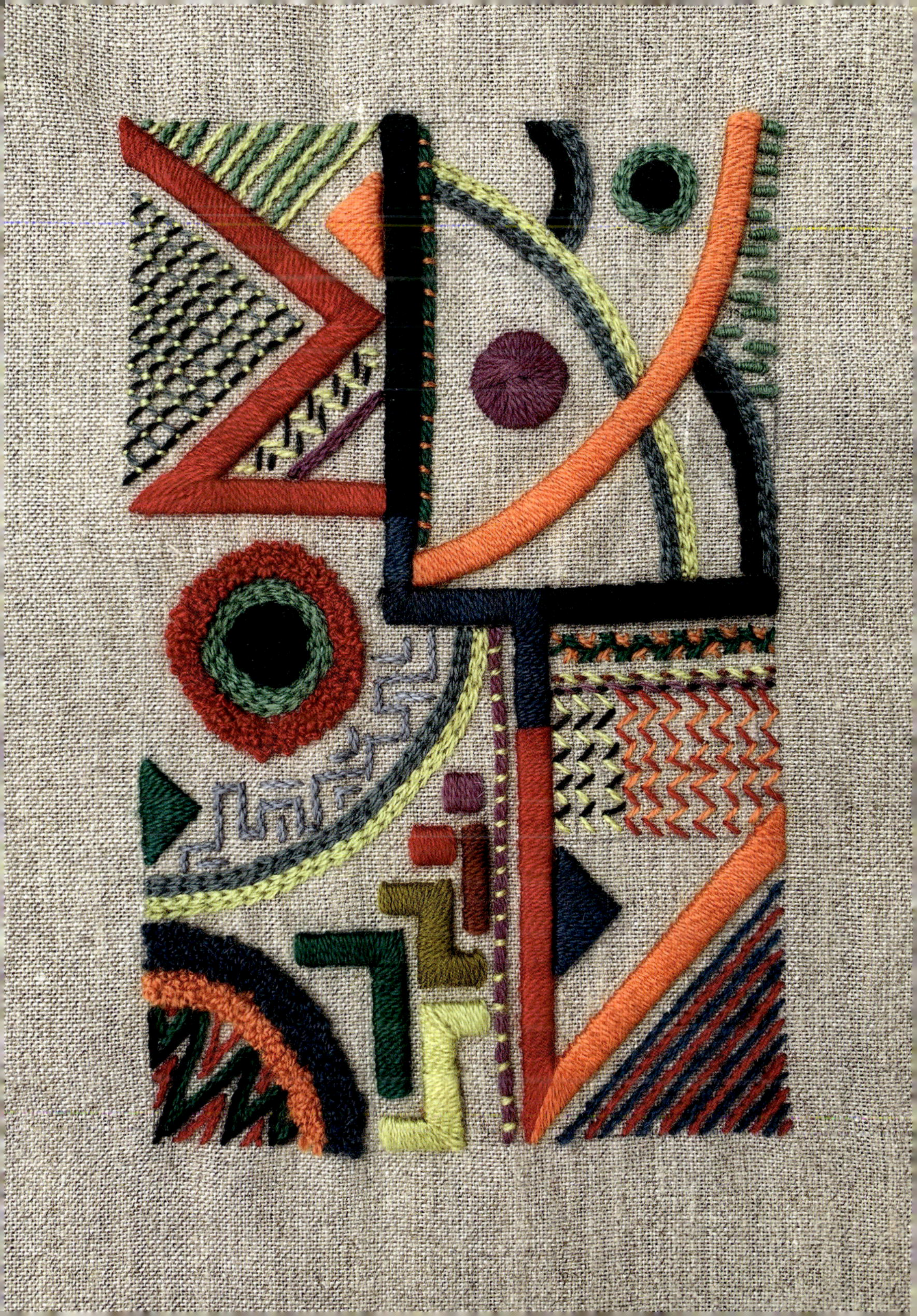

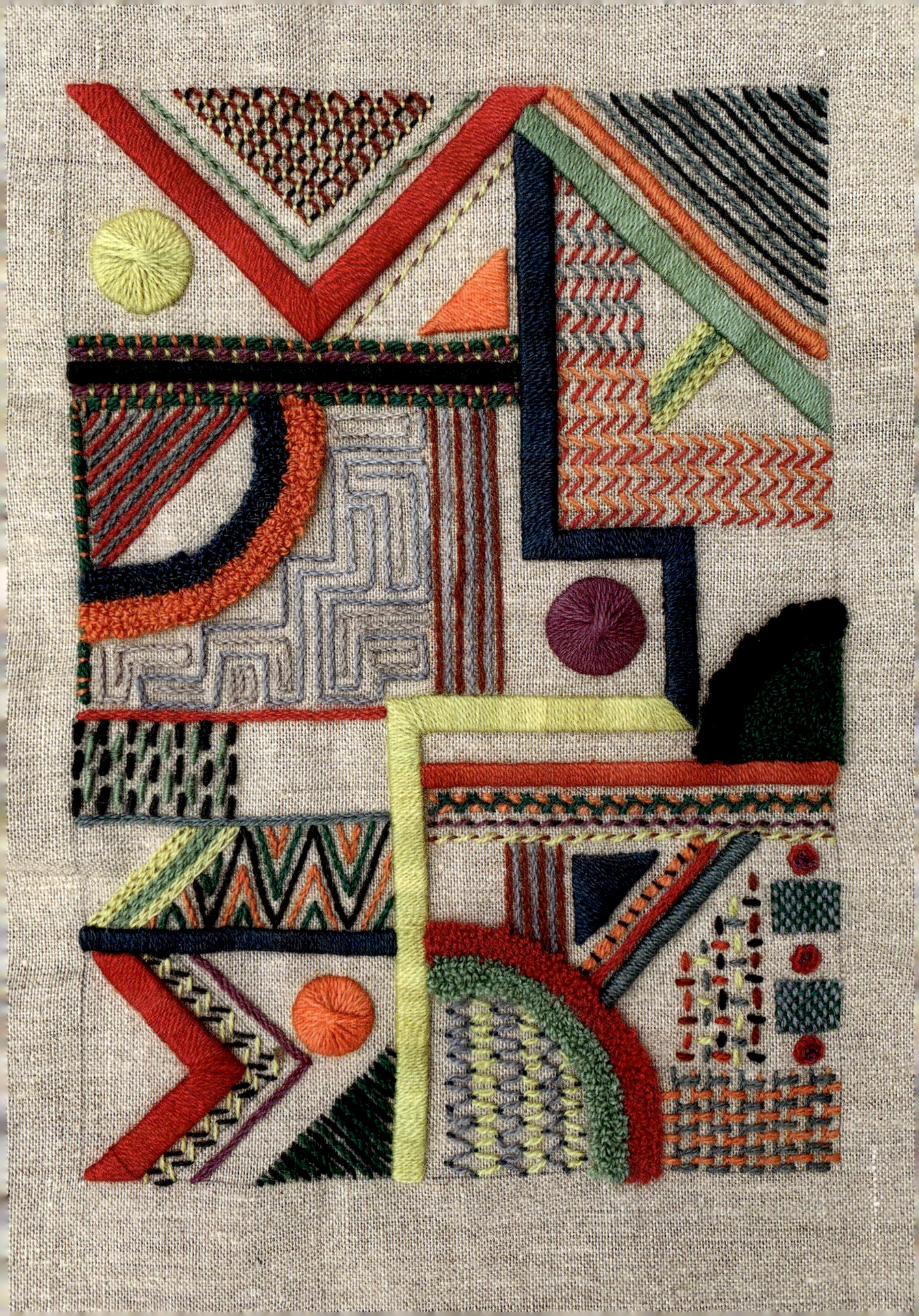

DOC DRUMHELLER

Shengze Haiku

silk and poetry
in the local dialect
both mean the same thing

at Shanghai airport
the bridge of rainbows connects
poets of the world

a Chinese poet
recites the famous Li Bai
playing drinking games

the sound of a drone
hovering above my head
dragonfly spy

the Chinese zither
sound of four winds in the wings
of a giant crane

polyester plant
all the workers leave at dusk
populate a town

pomegranate trees
grown at the ancient temple
remember the dead

woman at a loom
weaves the silken smiling face
of Happy Buddha

palindrome brocade
Su Hui wrote eight-inch poems
stitched in antique silk

reading the tea leaves
in the bottom of my cup
the future is green

modern miracle
how a silkworm is reborn
into a goddess

singing at midnight
a Mongolian song brings
life to centuries

RUTH CORKILL

Dioskouri

in the dark
garden party
full of tea lights
at the home
of a wealthy friend
someone asked were we
performance art

we had only eyes
ears and arms
for each other
rustled and chuckled
in one reticulation
had to admit we liked
the ambiguity of being
'Greek twins'
draped in warm stars

mocking around museum
cases bound arm in
arm Castor and Pollux
of the intune palms, forearms
pressed to the elbow
my mother came
into the exhibition
after us, warned
everyone is staring at you two.

SHAUN BAMBER

Our Son

Our son is a man of simple pleasures.
Butter on toast, spread right to the edges, melting away to nothing.
Grass under bare feet—no shoes for this boy.
A marble in his hand, warm and smooth, inner colours gleaming.
Hanging from a tree, teasing his sisters—but no more than absolutely necessary.
Striking through the water like a fish, brown skin glistening.
Hours spent reading—of dragons, wizards, a superhero or two.
Starchy crisp white sheets, fresh and cool against his limbs.
A spoonful of ice cream for a throat that's hot and dry.
The sun on his face, a comfortable spot to rest.
His mother's arms around him.
Butter on toast, spread right to the edges, melting away to nothing.
Our son was a man of simple pleasures.

KEITH NUNES

The Check-up

The doctor asked me at what age I experienced menarche, so I guessed what he meant because I'm no linguist, and told him when I had sex for the first time, which was seventeen, and he grimaced, then he clarified/emphasised that he meant when did I first menstruate, so I said thirteen, and he grinned as though I'd passed the test and I could now go home, which of course I couldn't because he wanted to rank my prolapse from one to four, four meaning *oh fuck, I'm going to have it all out*, and one meaning he'll tell me to do some Kegel exercises and it should clear up, as though I picked up a rash from weeding the wrong plant.

After withdrawing his thankfully small fingers, removing his gloves and providing a paper towel for me to wipe off the river of lubricant, he said, 'Well, Miz Davis, it would seem you are situated at the lower end of the prolapse ranking, meaning some Kegel exercises should clear things up rather well.'

My first reaction was to say *thank you* but for some unknown reason I said, 'Oh, marvellous', in an uncharacteristically sarcastic tone, which prompted that grimace again, and then, having pulled up my knickers and restored my dignity, I shocked us both by punching his shoulder like some bloke as I walked out.

MEDB CHARLETON

Desiring Fireflies

I wake in the purple dark
unable to land on word or phrase,
no crossings at this time
and the last ferry departed
but something draws me in, or out:
fireflies leaping like Olympic divers—
they must have come through
an open window in the house,
it being soft enough about—
I become a little conscious
and move my waking dream
across the floor to look
and still they loop and fleck the dark
with vaulting, pirouetting sparks—
'Come and see,' I call,
but when you rise, those tiny things,
novenas from a cavernous spring,
fall back towards the electric light.
I was a little wrong this time
but rightly still I see
the glint of their floating forms
and what a glimpse of beauty
before the world switched on.

DAVID EGGLETON

Afterlife

I would dig a bigger slice of the roseate
radiance that spins elusive in a pink cloud
beyond my fingertips, but as someone
slips and slides from the ski-slope every day,
headed for the biggest boulder around,
so my immortal soul turns the corkscrew
to an afterlife of booze and cigarettes
with hammered skin and the skull knuckled.
I make promises to the rock of ages,
then break it up to pave the planet.
Your otter skin pelt skims through the glittery
browed sea on a trip beyond me.
I drop like a sparrowhawk on a pigeon,
or spider on wasp, run like a Norway rat
up a limb to a forking dilemma and fall.
I have swum with the green sea turtle,
pondered a Victorian table,
and questioned the biblical fable
till it reared up and flew back to bite me,
who was unvaccinated and turned rabid.
I raged like a loon against the hideous moon
that glowed like a spoon over a lamp
to bubble tar, and drew up my blood
into a quasar doused with helium;
the resultant explosion lit the stars
and kept me staring into space
just twelve steps below paradise.

LEANNE RADOJKOVICH

Hailman

Mum and I caught the bus to visit Aunty Joyce on Saturday mornings. The last time it was winter, the cold made ringworms on my thighs.

There were huge sooty clouds overhead that crashed and sparked, thunder roared. We got out of the bus and wind whooshed my skirt. Leaves skittered along the gutter then a sandwich board crashed onto the footpath. We hurried to Joyce's; I held Mum's hand tight. Joyce wasn't my real aunty—Mum and Joyce weren't sisters—but I called her Aunty out of manners. Whenever we visited, she was mending or making gowns for ballroom dancing—liquid fabrics, shimmering falls of sequins. She'd talk with pins in the side of her mouth; when the pins ran out she fitted a cigarette into a holder and lit up. She let me play with her offcuts. I felt her glances. *If looks could kill*—of course they couldn't, but they could brush against the back of your neck, they could caress your cheek.

That morning we'd waited on the porch for Joyce. The temperature plunged between one knock and the next. There was a strange hush as if clouds were sucking up air; then hail shot down. The smell of knives burst from the concrete path. The door opened and Mum pushed me inside. Hail crackled against windows. Joyce dashed down the hall and opened the back door. Pellets popped and clumped onto the patio. I squeezed past Aunty Joyce and crouched down to touch the magic I'd never seen before. Never seen snow either.

'Come back,' Mum called.

'Let her enjoy it,' Joyce crouched beside me. We were both getting wet; her mascara smudged and a crumb dribbled down her face in a black tear.

Joyce and I began squashing hail into a mound until there was a soccer ball. 'It needs a head,' she said. We scooped together a smaller ball and plonked it on top. 'A snowman!' I squealed. 'A hailman!' I snapped off dandelion flowers for eyes and a geranium twig for a nose. Joyce pulled brass buttons from her pocket and poked them into the face until the hailman smiled. I watched her hands, just like mine, narrow fingers slim as chopsticks. Her wrists had the same bony knob on the side. I felt queasy and leant against the wall.

Joyce felt my gaze and caught it. Her pale eyes darkened. They made me think of the steel mirrors in school loos where all you can see is your shadow. She stood up and whisked down the hall. Mum tried to pull me inside but I wouldn't leave the hailman.

The popping stopped and turned into rain. The hailman began melting. Half his body sheared away and the head rolled off. Soon he was only a puddle. I picked up the brass buttons and slipped them into my pocket.

TONY BEYER

To Flute Music

I never lose interest
in the strange

three-dimensional calligraphy
of eels in the creek

even the thickest of them
seems able to bend

into any character
of an arcane alphabet

then as suddenly
the page they have inscribed

is wiped clean
by the shadow of the bank

WES LEE

Suddenly the Moon

Lying there in the ridiculous hat that looked like
you were about to take a shower,
I didn't think you would come back
when they wheeled you away and
I walked behind
until I could go no further with the smiling nurses.
I sat in your empty room
holding all my possessions and yours
in the backpack.
The metal frame of the bed appeared and then your face,
still in the ridiculous hat,
your eyes staring right at me,
gigantically wide,
larger than I had ever seen,
as if there was no one else there,
as if I was the only
thing you had ever seen and would see again.
As if I was suddenly the moon and you had been
let out into the night and someone had said *This*
is the last time you will ever see the moon.

OWEN MARSHALL

Frost Flowers

Wally Tamahana was captain of the first fifteen when I was in the fourth form, and famously told the headmaster to get off the fucken field. Becky Attwood was thrown from a steer at the Geraldine rodeo, broke her neck, but came right with time and ended up the chief of Work and Income. Alice Muirton went on a Rotary exchange to America and was killed by a lightning strike in Lincoln, Nebraska, after a high school prom. Barry Eldermere was bald at twenty-nine but became a multi-millionaire because of mānuka honey, while his more likeable brother, Albie, was jailed for corporate fraud, and Belinda Burge, who failed all her units at varsity, is now a worldwide celebrity as a creator of fashion hats and fascinators.

All of these people have a story, but I'm going to talk about Mrs Poole and Greg, who lived pretty quietly and hardly went anywhere when I knew them. We lived next door for quite a few years and got on well as neighbours. Mrs Poole's a widow, but her husband left her well provided for, as he'd been the main shareholder in a Lower Hutt factory making plastic guttering. She was small and thin when I first knew her, and both attributes became accentuated as the years passed. Her movements were staccato, as if clockwork provided her propulsion. A smart little woman, always well dressed and never without makeup. I got to know all of her children: Erin, who's married to a biology lecturer at Massey University; Sue, a parliamentary journalist; and Greg, who was disabled and lived with his mother.

I'm not sure what the matter was with Greg, but he couldn't walk, had awkward arm movements and his speech was difficult to understand. I've always assumed it was some problem at his birth. He could laugh though, and I liked to hear that. We could hear his laugh even from next door: explosive, deep and unrestrained. Less frequently we heard him crying, and that too was loud, and equally affecting in a quite different way.

When I was still at primary school Mrs Poole often invited me over to have a game of draughts with him. I took it as a compliment, and never thought that maybe he had no better, or more willing, company than a kid some ten years younger than himself. I still think it was more than that, though.

They both made me welcome. I remember winter weekend afternoons spent sitting with them in the warmth of the nearby woodburner. Milo and afghan biscuits, TV movies sometimes. Greg was good at draughts, although he tended to scatter the pieces. I think he let me win more times than I deserved.

In later years I took him for walks; well, I walked and pushed Greg in his wheelchair. He never did have an electric one and I don't know the reason for that: certainly it can't have been financial. In the year before I went to varsity I remember quite a few walks. I'd like to say they were always the result of spontaneous consideration on my part, but my mother often made the suggestion. It wasn't a drag, though, and I was happy to do it. Greg must have been nearly thirty then, but because of his dependence and limited experience of the world he seemed much younger, despite his encroaching baldness and hairy arms. His thin legs were always aligned the same way in the chair, rigidly together and slanted to the right. He would grip the armrests when we crossed a gutter, lean back to look at me and chortle if I did anything at speed. The park was his favourite destination, especially the playground where he could watch the little kids' antics, and the pond where the black swans presided over a scrabble of lesser birds. There was a bench by the silver birches that caught the sun nicely and I'd sit there with Greg's chair pulled up alongside. We'd talk a bit, which wasn't always easy because of his garbled words, but we weren't uncomfortable with silence.

One of the first times we went was a Sunday soon after Anzac Day. I remember because Greg still had two fabric poppies pinned to his green jersey and when I asked him why two and why still, he said they were for lost great-uncles. It was a blue, windless afternoon and people had been drawn to the park: families at the pond's edge feeding the ducks and swans, young people with frisbees or soccer balls, strolling couples.

One pair came slowly past from the direction of the old band rotunda. The guy was self-consciously casual, endeavouring to disguise his pride at accompanying such a good-looking girl. She really was a stunner: Hollywood legs in red shorts. There seemed a slight vibration in the air around her. When they'd gone on, Greg turned his head towards me in his ungainly way and said slowly, 'Wow, now she was something. Jesus.'

Yes, Jesus, she was something, but it seemed strange coming from Greg, and I realised that I had made the stupid assumption that because of his disability he didn't have the same responses and feelings as the rest of us. Why shouldn't he see a beautiful woman and think of taking her in his arms?

Why shouldn't he see a white mountain slope and imagine himself skiing there, regard the quivering sea and visualise the plunge into it, or watch a craftsman create something of balanced perfection and wish to share that satisfaction? Why must he accept the full imposition of such a savagely limited life before he had done anything at all to deserve it? You don't get any guarantee of a fair deal, do you?

Greg went on set days to a sheltered workshop, had for years, even played wheelchair basketball for a while, but his condition deteriorated steadily. The last few times I spent with him everything about him seemed to end on a slant, no matter which way I propped him up, and he talked less, perhaps because he'd become more difficult to understand.

He died during exam time in my second year in Auckland and I didn't get down for the funeral, but when I came home for vacation work at the woolstore I went over to see his mother.

A blustery, warm Friday with shrubs convulsing and shadows dancing. 'He liked you,' Mrs Poole said as I followed her into the sitting room. The photos of her husband and of Sue, Erin and Greg were still on the sideboard by the woodburner, but there was a new reminder of her son. His wheelchair by the window, and propped on its seat a large, framed image of him, smiling his slanted smile. It was to become a sort of memorial, the wheelchair and photograph, always there.

'He used to ask about you,' she said. 'He knew all the subjects you were taking and how you got on. He would have loved the opportunity to go to university himself. He started a polytech course offering preparation for academic study, but became too debilitated to continue.' Mrs Poole got up as she said this, went to the wheelchair and adjusted the photo frame in her clockwork way, just as she habitually used to help Greg change position there a little for greater ease. 'You liked to hear him, didn't you,' she said, going back to her green armchair.

'Hear him?'

'You told me once you and your mother liked to hear him laugh.'

'Right, yes we did, even from next door. It was pretty loud, wasn't it?'

'One of the workshop supervisors mentioned his laugh at the funeral.'

'*The Simpsons*,' I said. 'He really loved that programme. We watched it together sometimes.'

'He understood the social and political satire behind it. He knew it wasn't just cartoons. He knew a lot more than he could be bothered saying.'

'I remember us playing draughts too.'

'So do I,' she said.

'It can't have been easy.'

'Looking after him?'

'Yeah. Everything that had to be done, especially when he grew up.'

'Everyone said I should put him in care, even Erin and Sue, though they loved him. Everyone said it was too much for me and not the best choice for him either, but I couldn't do it, and he didn't want to go.' Mrs Poole leant forward from her armchair and lowered her voice, an unconscious emphasis of significance to come, rather than to ensure privacy, because we were quite alone. 'He knew we wouldn't have that long together. "I won't make old bones," he used to say. He knew all right, and so did I.'

Mrs Poole was of a different generation to me, and a different gender, and I was a bit surprised by her openness, the honesty with which she spoke to me of Greg, the equality she assumed I felt. I suppose it was because there weren't many people she could talk to who remembered him. She was a well-educated woman and unconventional in her own way. She wasn't swayed by others.

Even after I left home permanently I used to go over to see Mrs Poole if I was back visiting my parents. The wheelchair was always there, and Greg in his frame. I knew she loved all her children, but for her son there was a sense of fulfilment lacking, for which she held herself unaccountably responsible.

On my last visit, before she moved to Palmerston North to live with Erin, she told me as much. We were on her deck, out of sight of the wheelchair and Greg's image, with a view of her large, well-kept garden, which she no longer needed to maintain. My mother was envious. Lot and lots of peonies with their large, roundly compact heads, already tinctured with a range of colours, ready to burst into flower. Mrs Poole made a point of congratulating me on my marriage—her generous gift had been a small inlaid Italian table—and she was interested in my work at the ministry. We came round of course to talk of Greg, for that was the bond we shared. 'Towards the end,' she said, after we had been talking for some time, 'he had this thing about frost flowers. Did I ever tell you about that?'

'I don't think so.'

'He watched this nature programme that featured them—fragile petals and stems of pure ice that form and grow when certain plants become frozen. Very strange and very beautiful, and very rare. He really wanted to see them and we began to plan a trip overseas, although we both knew it wouldn't happen.

'We made up a full itinerary and he had pictures of frost flowers on his wall. He could have been a scientist if he'd had the chance. He never blamed me, but you can't help thinking what might have been, can you? What you might have done differently.'

It was odd, and rather sad, that last conversation with Mrs Poole: sitting in the sun with a view of the profusion of peonies and talking of frost flowers, and what life might have been for Greg if he'd been given a chance. It made me realise that the love of a mother for her child is incalculable in its intensity, unassailable in its loyalty, unbearable in any perceived betrayal.

CAROLYN McCURDIE

I Forgot to Mention Ecclesiastes 3

I claim no part except neglect, my failure to weed, prune or clip, that has let
spring lollop through my garden with the tail-swinging, tongue-flopping,
blind-with-joy heedlessness of several litters of puppies. So I was kind
to the two young Bible-toting women who'd pushed through the poor
    discipline
and knocked, snagged and bloodied, at my door.

I reminded myself that they'd risked my front path to save me.
And the rescue they brought was extreme. Summing up my wrinkles,
they promised that God will lift my corpse out of my grave, lift everyone up:
my loved ones, every person to draw breath since Adam and—they made
    clear—
this was not a metaphor.

It wasn't the first time I'd been offered this promise—I've been old for a
    while—
and previously I'd argued: Everyone? So a tighter, more sweaty jostle
on this already burdened planet?
Foolish, perhaps, when for them, no speckle's allowed on the gloss of belief:
God can do anything. Would I like to hear the verse from the Bible?

This time I had backup. A rampant rose leaned over the step so that one
woman had to stand sideways to escape the thorns. There's a transmutation
of golden light deep in the whorl where the pink petals meet and this small
warmth spilled into the talk. Maybe that was the difference, or maybe the
    weeds,
the thistles and dandelions, out of place, impolite, elbowing in.

I found myself singing the praises of death. There's beauty, I said, in the interstitching
of life and death, fraternal twins each creating the other.
Decay builds the soil that feeds plants, feeds all that walk, crawl, fly.
A series of deaths makes my morning coffee and toast. One woman nodded,
but between us, their chapter and verse, pulled down like the slats of a blind.

Then my own words did that magical thing, no longer rant or argument
but off with a life of their own, and I the witless listener, not knowing where I'd be led.
I heard myself say that death is a process of giving. What's a gift? It's an act of love
and when I die and decay I'll be coffee and toast for a tree perhaps, or a shrub—
I waved my hand at the greening hydrangea, leaves quaffing sunlight to kindle
a summer of colour, a promise of bouquets, blues, pinks and reds.

My verbal flight drove them back down the path. I smiled my goodbyes, with the rose
there beside me, glad that the women had pricked me, provoked me,
glad for what arrives unexpected with age—the changing perspectives,
the shift, and then shift, of the light.

CHARLOTTE STEEL

Patearoa

a failed goldminer built his dam here, at the end
of the known tracks, where the hills burn and crumple
like dry paper, where a yellowhammer sits like an effigy
on the bridge, its metal squealing
returning the song

and the sky is like a bowl, like something
glass, like a beckoning, open
to the winds

it is something to see out of

the miner's brother built his house further down
the river, at the elbow of the current,
his dogs in a stone kennel, cairns of rock

the water never clearer
no weed, or algae

a convict lived in the paddocks on the other side
a trifling offence, a life under rocks and canvas,
the only respite from the cold
the warmth of drink

at the races, the foreign miners placed bets
while small boys snuck behind them
to hear another language

the horses pass
the dust they leave reaches
up into the sky, and fades
like so many lives upon the wind.

MALINNA LIANG

Archipelago

Andy arrives late enough for Evelyn to answer the door in a kimono. 'The boys have whiskey and rosé,' she says instead of hello. 'And Josif will give you heroin if you slip him tongue.'

Josif, a Serbian business major in a bohemian arrangement with Evelyn, is mixing a Long Island iced tea in a pilsner. He says, 'Not interested.'

All around the lounge is the detritus of a drinking game, and as soon as Andy puts her bag down it becomes apparent that the whiskey and rosé must wait, because Willa has her face stuffed into the crack of the couch.

'Oh Jesus.' Evelyn, laughing, helps Andy haul Willa to her feet and they stumble past the kitchen, down the hall, through the second door on the left, and lay her on Evelyn's California King. 'Sleeping Beauty,' Evelyn says, as Andy tucks Willa in. She can tell from her dead weight and the way her eyes do not move under her lids that Willa is blacked out, slot-machining, and must have been the loser in whatever game they played.

'Nuh uh,' Evelyn says at the look on Andy's face. 'I didn't make her keep drinking.'

Andy wonders not for the first time if Evelyn actually likes Willa, or if their friendship consists purely of unfulfilled mutual sexual attraction and the type of envy girls who wear heels feel for girls who don't wear makeup. 'Aren't you glad I don't want to sleep with you?' Evelyn used to say to her before Willa became a regular at the loft.

Andy says, 'Let's go outside.'

An hour later, four rounds in, they sit on the balcony with the boys, drinking whiskey and rosé, bitching about the vice-chancellor, wondering out loud if they could crack an A+ in Contract by giving Professor Franklin head. Curtis and Ron both say they'd do it, sure, for an A+. Curtis adds, 'I'm not a homophobe.'

In the safety of Evelyn's loft this conversation feels transgressive instead of embarrassing, very urban, and only slightly hollow. It's the sort of dialogue Andy might script then abandon, half plagiarising from a television show she scoffs about to friends but binges in private. How many thousands of girls her age across the globe are having this exact conversation? A secret society of people who pirate the same show? Has anything Andy ever said not been said before, and better?

Evelyn says, 'I know you're doing shit in Contract.'

'I got a B+.'

'That's not bad,' Curtis says. Ron laughs.

Andy says, 'He looks like Santa Claus.'

'You wouldn't be looking at his face.'

'Ugh,' Ron says. 'If you guys stay on Franklin's ballsack, I'm gonna go.'

Evelyn just smiles. 'Where're you gonna go, Ron?'

Ron darkens. 'All right, all right,' Curtis says as he waves a bottle of rosé around. He doesn't find rosé emasculating. 'It tastes good and it's got alcohol in it,' he said to Andy once. 'And I own a pink shirt.'

And so it goes. Andy drinks her whiskey and taps off ash from her cigarette, which she has bummed. She only smokes when she drinks—not because she particularly enjoys the taste or the effect, but because it makes her feel like an adult.

'Curtis got assaulted last week at the Long Room,' Evelyn tells Andy.

'What?'

Curtis sips his rosé. 'Some lady grabbed my dick.'

Ron says, 'Congrats.'

Curtis doesn't look bothered, so Andy says, 'You should write a piece about it for the magazine.'

Evelyn laughs into her drink. 'I'd run it.' She is an editor this year. 'A MILF Grabbed My Dick in the Long Room and Why Going Home with Her is Direct Action.'

'You what?'

Curtis shrugs.

Ron says, 'Hashtag MeToo.'

'Piss off.'

'Oh please,' Evelyn says. 'You bloody left me at the bar—you couldn't leave quick enough.'

'I feel like there are steps she could have taken before that. You know, the—' Andy gestures.

Evelyn mimics her. 'The what? Show us how you'd do it.'

Andy feels red, but she obliges and makes a grabbing motion again, tighter this time, until her hand closes into a fist. Evelyn cackles. Ron grabs at his crotch, mimes a rupturing. Curtis smiles uncomfortably.

At times like these, Andy thinks, it feels nice to have someone else who tires of Evelyn's Woodstock fever, Evelyn's arrangements, Evelyn's parade of girls, none as blue-haired or pierced as Andy always expects lesbians to be, all incredibly thin, wearing cashmere and expensive scarfs, rolling their own cigarettes. Some of us, Andy always wants but never dares to say, aren't as evolved as you.

She needs to stop hating Evelyn in private. It's cowardly.

'But anyway,' Evelyn says, 'we can't talk about these things in front of her,' looking at Andy. To Ron: 'She's a virgin.'

'Jesus,' Andy says. 'Evelyn.'

'What?'

'Really?'

It feels like the first time Ron has ever looked at her instead of through. Andy feels a prickling under her skin, the blood buzzing there. She sees nothing out of the corners of her eyes—not the lights of the loft, or Curtis's face, or the black water in the Viaduct. Only the sensation of being looked at, so she looks away.

'Any particular reason?'

Evelyn says, 'She's Catholic.'

'Catholics are sluts.'

'I'm *not* Catholic,' Andy says.

'What are you then?'

'I think it's arrogant for anyone to pretend to know for sure.'

'No,' Ron gestures. 'Is it, like, a cultural thing or—'

'It's not a cultural thing. I'm going to check on Willa.'

'Stay a bit,' Ron says.

'Yeah,' Evelyn parrots. 'Stay a bit.'

Evelyn is cruel only on special occasions: after Josif tells mutual friends they are dating, after arguments with her father, or sometimes, less often now, after she has to go out in her shortest dress and look for lonely men wearing Cartier watches. All sympathetic reasons, which grant her an authority to be cruel beyond what Andy tolerates from others, even herself. But tonight she feels like a beached whale: defenceless, dead, children poking at her bloated stomach with sticks.

Curtis says nothing.

Evelyn continues. 'She doesn't even masturbate.'

'*Really?*'

Andy stands up. 'I'm checking on Willa.'

'Oh don't,' Evelyn protests. 'We're joking. It's a joke!' Then, because she can't resist, 'We'll show you how!' Cackling. So Andy keeps going. Up the wooden steps, swaying and black; she smells the putrid water beneath, and when she reaches the top she flicks the butt of her cigarette over the ledge and into the water. She had been holding it all this time but had forgotten to smoke it.

Later, after she makes herself throw up, the cigarette smell will cling to the collar of her shirt and the ends of her hair, little molecules of carcinogen pretending to be menthol. The smell will make her sick, so she will need to throw up again.

In the lounge, Evelyn's Korean roommate Dani has just come back from her lab and now lies on the couch, scrolling through her phone. 'When are you all leaving?'

'We might stay the night.'

'Ugh.'

'How's Willa?'

'She's sleeping it off.'

'Yeah, I know,' Andy says. 'Thanks.'

Evelyn's CBD apartment is a divorce-settlement gift from her father, sleekly and impersonally furnished, the fridge always empty of everything but cold brew, wine and protein shakes. It has three bedrooms, of which Evelyn's is the only ensuite. A week ago Evelyn confided in Andy that a Dutch ex of hers was in Auckland for holiday, so Josif was strictly *persona non grata* in her bedroom, on pain of permanent deportation. Josif hadn't taken it well. 'That's what Dani's here for,' Evelyn had said. 'Josif can't make a scene because Dani would talk, and he cares so much about talk.'

Evelyn's bedroom door is closed. Andy knocks. 'You okay?'

There is a shuffling inside.

Josif's voice: 'We're fine.'

Andy looks at her hand on the doorknob. Her fingers tighten, then go loose. She sees the pink accent on her white knuckles where they flex. 'Is Willa in there?'

'She's fine,' says Josif.

'Okay.'

Andy begins to walk away. The inside of her stomach is hot and liquid, roiling in waves, but her neck is cold. She has a flashing, gory thought about the alcohol in her belly souring into vinegar, then time-lapsing through a chemical process of calcification, becoming a solid mass heavy enough to drop her through the floor into the dirty water beneath and keep going until she settles in the centre of the earth, under ten thousand kilometres of firmament and silt.

Andy stops and looks back at the door. 'Willa?' She calls again, louder. 'Willa?'

There is nothing for a handful of enormous seconds. Then the soft sound of Josif's feet on the carpet, a padding, nearly animal, as he makes his way to the door. Andy lurches forward and opens the door to a dark room, darker than the hall.

Josif says, 'I was just going to open it.'

He is shirtless. The faded waistband of his briefs proclaims CALVIN KLEIN CALVIN KLEIN CALVIN KLEIN. He smells like nothing in particular, which is worse than if he did. He looks sleepy, rubbing his eyes as if he'd just woken up.

Behind him in the bed, Willa is asleep on her side. She still has her dress on.

'You okay?' Josif asks Andy.

'Yeah, fine.'

Josif gives her a confused smile, a little boy's smile, the smile that must have made his mother fall in love, and closes the door on her. Andy thinks about knocking again, about saying, 'Wait, wait, wait', but she can't make herself move. When she put Willa to bed two hours ago it had been in that same position, but had her shoes been on or off? Her hair up or down? She can't remember. Go in, go on, make a scene, come on. Come on. Come on.

But it's Josif. I know him.

'Hey.' Curtis is at the end of the hall. 'Is she okay?'

Andy feels her limbs come back to life. See? We know each other. I know Josif like I know Curtis.

'I think she drank too much.'

'She always drinks too much.'

'So do you.'

'I've got thirty centimetres on her. And I can still walk to the stop and catch the last bus.'

'You're not staying?'

'I am. Did she throw up?'

'A while ago.' Andy struggles, then blurts, 'Josif's in there.'

Curtis looks at her and makes an expression with his eyebrows. 'Oh.' He gives a quick laugh, then says, 'Oh, okay.' Laughs again.

Andy goes into the bathroom. Curtis follows. The counter is covered in expensive skincare, SKII and La Mer, brands Andy can never justify buying even with her dad's credit card, even though he never checks the statements. There are tangles of long hair on the ground, like birds' nests.

Andy keeps her voice low. 'Do you think I should ...'

He waits for her to finish. She doesn't. 'I'm not a girl,' he says.

'Do you have to be a girl?'

'I'd leave my mate in there. But that's me. That's,' he laughs again and says, in Evelyn's voice, 'toxic masculinity, or whatever.'

Toward the end of the last semester, when Evelyn had been too busy with her advocacy work to come out on the weekends, it had been just Andy, Curtis, Willa and an annoying girl from Andy's Roman Warfare class named Bethany, whom they befriended accidentally. After drinks one night they stumbled from the student bar to Andy's apartment, where there was only one bed. The four of them lay down on it, Andy close to passing out, her head in Bethany's lap. She listened to the other three argue about the upcoming election, proposed housing cuts, whether or not Willa would ever sleep with that libertarian MP she interviewed for the magazine. The interview had consisted of twenty eight questions which were designed by a psychologist to make anyone fall in love with anyone, and at the end of it Willa had found the libertarian surprisingly palatable.

Does he prefer *The Fountainhead* or *Atlas Shrugged*? Andy had asked. She had never read either and neither had any of the others, but they all knew libertarians loved Ayn Rand. So they laughed, in on the same cleverness. They were clever. People often said so.

'What if you went in with me to check on her?' Andy asks. 'I'll just be like, "Oh, so this is where the party is?"'

Curtis laughs and mimics her. 'Oh, so this is where the party is? Who talks like that?'

'Americans.'

'Americans in movies.'

After a while the bed had begun to float and Curtis and Willa were kissing. 'Wow,' Bethany said. 'Drinks with a show.' It was the only time Bethany had ever made Andy laugh in the entire time they knew each other, and she saw Curtis smile at the corner of his mouth where he was still kissing Willa.

Afterwards Curtis and Willa walked Bethany back to her building and Andy lay in bed, alone at last, floating in that amniotic space between awake and asleep, willing herself to get up and vomit, listening to the sounds that lingered in the room like ghosts. Slick, wet. The next morning she got up and stripped her sheets. Two days later Evelyn said, 'Apparently Willa's tits are insane.'

Andy reaches for a bottle of micellar water and a cotton round and begins to take off her makeup. Her blocky eyebrows, her heavy liner, her mascara and foundation, all of it suddenly too unbearable to tolerate on her skin, even as Curtis still stands there watching her. She wants to scratch it off with her nails until she is clean again, even if she has to be naked in front of him, even if she has to be looked at.

Under the makeup she looks even drunker. Patches of blotchiness bloom across her cheeks, illuminating a few zits into furious fluorescence. She looks ugly, and worse, she looks young.

'We can, if you want,' Curtis says.

'You don't think it's weird?'

'Andy,' he sighs and leans down, so his cheek presses against hers. They look at themselves in the mirror. 'Don't make me say what Evelyn would say.'

'You don't know what Evelyn would say.'

'Then why didn't you go in there?'

Because I don't know how any of this shit works. Because I hate being laughed at. Because the longer I stand out here talking circles with you the more time goes by, and the less reason I have to go in because whatever has happened has happened. Because I know you people talk.

'You look better like this,' Curtis says suddenly. 'You look good.'

After the talk about the libertarian but before the kissing, conversation had turned to Evelyn. 'I know you're curious,' Curtis said to Willa, who just laughed.

'So you guys do this?' Bethany had asked. 'This is, like, cool and normal?'

'It happens sometimes,' Willa replied, nearly apologetic. 'But it's cool.'

'Is it?' Bethany asked. 'I mean, really?'

Andy's eyes were closed. 'Jeez,' she heard Curtis say. 'It just happens.' Willa was laughing. 'We're friends, and sometimes things just happen. It's all—mutual. Right?'

'Oh, so you would too?' Bethany asked Andy. She made a sluggish okay sign, which made Curtis and Willa laugh. 'Hm,' she said, pretending to be drunker than she was, pretending she couldn't hear them. She imagined she was floating in a pool with her ears under the surface.

'You're not my type, sorry,' Willa had said.

Andy had said, 'Bitch.'

'And you?' Bethany asked Curtis.

'I mean, yeah,' Curtis had said. 'I'd go down on you, Andy.'

She watches herself blink in the mirror. The glass that separates her from her reflection tosses her out of sync, so that she opens her eyes half a second before her reflection does, and in that half-second she sees her own closed eyelids, the red spiderwebs under pale skin. She sees herself as Curtis sees her, as Evelyn sees her: scrambling and small, consumed by a pathetic fear she can barely explain to herself. Brave enough to open the door and look inside but too afraid to go in. She wavers on the threshold, looking in, always looking in, even as someone is shutting the door. Then she blinks and steps back inside herself, and finds herself saying, 'Maybe I'll just wait a bit before I go in.'

Curtis presses his nose into her cheek. Andy watches her own slow stupid eyes, the pupils wide. There is a prickling at the back of her neck, which she realises a moment later is his lapel.

After he'd said that, she had laughed. That was the funniest thing she'd ever heard him say. Do you remember when …? she nearly said now, but kept her mouth closed. How long ago was it now? How long ago was my flat-warming?

A small party, to celebrate Andy moving into town. Just the four of them; always the four of them, mirrors in a funhouse. Then, Evelyn was with Josif proper. Before the front door had shut, Andy saw Josif's shadow through the sliding door that separated the lounge from the bedroom, and heard Evelyn's laughter when he said, 'You two have fun.' Then the bed had dipped beside her as Curtis lay down.

And they just left me. They just left me in there with you.

'I think I need to throw up,' Andy says now.

Curtis pushes his stubble against her jaw. 'Okay.'

IAIN BRITTON

foamdrunk@orientalbay

in the water the girl

strokes through burst white blood vessels & the white blood

congeals & drifts into small white land forms

foam drunk
she cavorts with gilled deities

& she being one of them   she with her aqueous tendencies

her smooth body

sucks on water beads
hydrates her veins in rock pools of light

she picks off scaly transparencies

eyes blurred   the girl with the godlook
paddles through stars

she calls for the trees to get into line   to ward off

prying spectators   she insists on preserving
times past   on holding them together   she treads water

while planets   pull ever forwards   ever apart

children with mothers traipse through sand
children with small luminous faces

mothers struggle with silhouettes

wanting to run

BRENT KININMONT

Child Carrier

Here comes another toddler with
a parent on their back
wading through the airshow crowd.

Did Toni Stadler train that way—
soft limbs fixed
in starfish formation—

before he became, aged four,
the youngest ever to tandem leap
from an aeroplane?

The footnote in the programme
does not elaborate.
His parents were raising

other questions, too.
About the minimum age,
and did they pretend it was play?

The jumpmaster a sheriff
perhaps, wearing their child
like a tin star

while out of respect for the law
of gravity the clouds
didn't hold them up.

RHYS FEENEY

200,000 dead chickens in a trenchcoat pretending to be a man

On or before 3 December 2019 around 190,000 chickens either suffocated or overheated when the ventilation system (and subsequently its backup and alarm system) failed at a Tegel-supplying chicken farm in Helensville. These chickens represent approximately 0.2% of the 96,820,000 chickens killed in Aotearoa each year.

200,000 chickens in a trenchcoat walk into a bar
in helensville & order a pint of export gold
the bartender asks if they watched the melbourne cup
& 400,000 wings draw tighter around 400,000 lungs
so that there is no room for a gasp to escape
a million feathers stand pressed together
as drops of condensation form on the pint glass
the beer does nothing to cool them down

200,000 chickens in a trenchcoat walk home alone
hilux after hilux passing with industrial-strength lights
that carve the landscape into ashen strips
the chickens bury their clipped beaks into their collars
you can't reveal that you're a prey animal
when walking home alone at night

the wind picks up &
200,000 chickens want to unfurl their trenchcoat
to let the fresh air brush over their bodies
to strip them of their fear
to remind them of their ancestors
feeling the force of the meteor impact

200,000 domesticated dinosaurs in a trenchcoat
sit down in front of the television
flick uncaring through ads for xmas dinner

200,000 chickens in a trenchcoat
smoke a durry on the deck
the smoke floats nebulous
the chickens make out shapes
barns / cages / chickens / eggs

200,000 chickens undo their trenchcoat
a pile of animal impulses disintegrates onto the bed

alone at night the chickens peck at each other
they need to talk to someone about this
how they take their anger out on the ones they love
but in helensville it is nearly impossible to get
a doctor's appointment
especially when you are 200,000 chickens
pretending to be a man

the mass of body heat that is 200,000 chickens in a double bed
shifts like an ocean that can't conceive of its own size
that can't imagine a future for itself where it is better
when the chickens log into twitter in the middle of the night
& see people surveying their past decade
they realise so much of their memory
has been lost in a daily routine
that they'll repeat when the sun rises

the chickens fall asleep holding their phone

JAMES NORCLIFFE

Penguin Modern Classics

Light the log burner. Let trees burn,
words burn. Keep yourself warm
this cold night. Open the damper.

The fire will roar. Draw the curtain
on the scarlet sky. Darkness is not
far away and neither is the frost.

Let the deceased descend from the shelf
and disport themselves on the table
beside a pot of freshly brewed coffee.

The letters form themselves into names
you know well but cannot really
know at all. Let them announce themselves.

Here we are, they whisper. Here we are
again. The same as we always were, but
different—as of course are you, dear reader.

You must forgive us for reminding you
of this. We cannot help being dog-eared,
fly-spotted and ever so slightly foxed

as are you, dear reader, as are you, even as
the fire goes out and the coffee grows cold.

The Landfall Review

Landfall Review Online

www.landfallreview.com

Reviews posted since October 2019
(reviewer's name in brackets)

October 2019

Everything's Something in Place by John Geraets (Mary Cresswell)
Contents Under Pressure by Gail Ingram (Mary Cresswell)
Lay Studies by Steven Toussaint (Mary Cresswell)
Attraction by Ruby Porter (Hannah Mettner)
Every morning, so far, I'm alive by Wendy Parkins (Emma Gattey)
The Boyfriend by Laura Southgate (Penelope Todd)
West Island by Stephanie Johnson (Lucy Sussex)

November 2019

McCahon Country by Justin Paton (Martin Edmond)
Whatever It Takes by John Reid (Helen Watson White)
This Thin Now by Jo Thorpe (Michael Steven)
Her Limitless Her by Reihana Robinson (Michael Steven)
Over There a Mountain by Elizabeth Welsh (Michael Steven)
Dead Letters by Jared Davidson (Briar Wood)
Fifteen Million Years in Antarctica by Rebecca Priestley (Briar Wood)
Working the Tang by Nicola Easthope (Lynn Jenner)
How I Get Ready by Ashleigh Young (Lynn Jenner)
Karl Wolfskehl by Friedrich Voit (Bill Direen)

December 2019

The Absolute Book by Elizabeth Knox (Octavia Cade)
Te Kōparapara, eds Suzanne Duncan et al. (Shirley Simmonds)
100 Days that Mapped a Nation by Graeme Lay (Tom Brooking)
Where We Land by Tim Jones (Rushi Vyas)
The Everrumble by Michelle Elvy (Rushi Vyas)
Soul Etchings by Sandra Arnold (Rushi Vyas)
Lost and Somewhere Else by Jenny Bornholdt (Lynn Davidson)
Moth Hour by Anne Kennedy (Lynn Davidson)
The Grief Almanac (Lynn Davidson)
Tutu Te Puehu, eds John Crawford and Ian McGibbon (Nicholas Reid)
New Zealand and the Sea (Nicholas Reid)

February 2020

All Who Live on Islands by Rose Lu (Nina Mingya Powles)
Scented by Laurence Fearnley (Elizabeth Heritage)
Wild Honey by Paula Green (Emer Lyons)
Waterline by Chris Else (Stephanie Johnson)
The Unreliable People by Rosetta Allan (Majella Cullinane)
The Nancys by R.W.R. McDonald (Vanda Symon)

March 2020

Auē by Becky Manawatu (Arihia Latham)
Making History by Jock Phillips (Helen Watson White)
Dandy Bogan by Nick Ascroft (Michael Steven)
Islander by Lynn Davidson (Michael Steven)
The Broken Estate by Mel Bunce (Giovanni Tiso)
Student Political Action in New Zealand by Sylvia Nissen (Giovanni Tiso)
The Dawnhounds by Sascha Stronach (Octavia Cade)
All of Us by Adrienne Jansen and Carina Gallegos (Renee Liang)
More of Us, eds Adrienne Jansen et al. (Renee Liang)

A Perpetually Stoned Hedgehog

Sarah Harpur

Funny As: The story of New Zealand comedy
by Paul Horan and Philip Matthews (Auckland University Press, 2019), 336pp., $50

Wrapped in his famous yellow towel, Billy T James grins at me from the cover of *Funny As*. I went to a rural school in 1980s New Zealand in a predominantly Pākehā farming community where we greeted each other by asking, 'How's the price of beef?' Yet Billy T James was our hero. At the time we were completely unaware of the criticism and scrutiny he faced. Who didn't adore Billy? No one I knew. When I was informed of my own Māori heritage, I pined to be Billy T's lost niece. Billy T James had a bad heart like my dad, and when he died it felt personal. Twenty-eight years later, we still wave when we drive past his resting place on Mt Taupiri.

Funny As starts with a dissection of one of his iconic sketches: 'Where did I get this bag? I pinched it.' It cleanly pulls apart the reasons why this sketch worked, the prejudices it confirmed, why it provoked criticism and why we still remember it today. It's painful to realise that our schoolyard laughter fuelled negative stereotypes. That we were not necessarily laughing for the reasons we thought. But that is what this book does so brilliantly: it shines a light on the attitudes of society at the time, from all corners of New Zealand. The comedy that finds success is a reflection of its audience.

Funny As is not just a chronological retelling of who did what and where; it is unflinching in its assessment of both the comedian and the audience. Although it can feel like a Maglite in the face, it is written with compassion rather than condemnation. For every person who felt uncomfortable about Billy T James's representation of Māori in New Zealand, there was another who was inspired to see a Māori man front and centre, making an extraordinary career for himself.

Our attitudes are constantly evolving: as we know better, we do better. It is from this non-hysterical place that we can see a way forward, to where a thriving creative scene creates stories *with* the cultural minority, not *about* them. To where the cultural minority are writers, directors, producers and actors of their own stories. *Funny As* argues for this without pandering or preaching.

I enjoyed learning more about the obvious success stories of New Zealand comedy, the household names and the familiar faces. Several comedians are the subject of their own chapter: alongside Billy T James are John Clarke, the Topp Twins, the Front Lawn, Flight of the Conchords and Taika Waititi. But for me, the added joy of this book was the discovery of more obscure voices, such as Ted Kavanagh, the Kiwi who wrote a BBC radio comedy that paved the way for *The Goon Show*; and wartime cartoonist David Low, whose unflattering depictions of Hitler caused his name to be added to the black book marked for arrest should Germany invade England. It makes me so happy that in the 1990s there was a troupe of lesbian comedians named 'Fanny Business', and that in the 1970s the *NZ Listener* published a cartoon starring a perpetually stoned hedgehog.

Like most forms of growth, the evolution of comedy is erratic. It is Einsteinian, not Newtonian. Paul Horan and Philip Matthews have created an engaging narrative accompanied by a wealth of images. It must have been a mammoth task to compile the hundreds of interviews, photos, cartoons and posters and plot these into a coherent order. It is an admirable feat.

So much of live performance is ephemeral, and comedy has long been thought to have minimal artistic value. The authors acknowledge the challenge of finding records of events which, at the time, were not considered worth archiving. Their research struggle reminds me of stories we heard at film school about the iconic New Zealand drama series *Gloss*, of which few episodes remain. According to legend, tapes were so expensive that after a programme was broadcast, the content was wiped and the tapes reused. I feel confident that any gaps in this book are not the result of a lack of effort. In the Introduction a vaudevillian performer talks about a hilarious and unknown 'Mrs Clark'. The authors note their frustration: 'We would've loved to tell more about the Mrs Clarks but often all that remained was a scrap of information. We hope that this story of New Zealand Comedy is a start.' It is a lot more than a start. Traversing through war, cabaret, literature, cartoons, theatre, politics, television, film and stand-up, there are heroes to be discovered and rediscovered on every page.

Comedy is usually confined to a section of an arts festival programme, a corner of a dying DVD store or a theatre basement, but *Funny As* allows a broader definition. Comedy is not so much the 'what' as the 'why'. Comedy is created to make sense of the world, and it feels better to laugh about misfortune or the hideous truth than to develop an ulcer.

I am glad this book was made. It is the book I did not know I needed, a social education as much as a history lesson. It is entertaining and feels good in your hands. The images are endlessly fascinating; the text is slick; and it can be enjoyed from a random starting point or read cover to cover.

Funny As accompanies a documentary series for TV1. While there is some crossover, each is an impressive work in its own right, and both make best use of their medium. While a book could never capture Lynn of Tawa's iconic twang, neither can the TV series allow you to linger over Rosemary McLeod's exquisite cartoons that are as cutting today as when first published in the 1970s. To discover a new hero like McLeod makes me feel like a teenager who thinks they discovered Pink Floyd. I am well aware that anyone older than me has probably been a fan for years, but I will never read McLeod's column again without saluting her.

Unlike the documentary series, there is no designated chapter on 'How Difficult It Must Have Been to Participate in Comedy if You Were Born with a Uterus'. That story is ever-present, especially if you read the book by pictures alone. There is an ache that accumulates when you flick through photo after photo of men in zany poses. How impenetrable this industry must have been for women, who were sometimes allowed to play, but not with the boys. I like to think it is better today, but the fact remains that we still live in a world where gender equality looks like a ratio of five men to two women on a 7 *Days* panel. I am happy that Michelle A'Court's experience of comedy in the 1990s was of 'nice boys no sleaze'. My own experience has also been overwhelmingly positive, but that is not the case for all women, many of whom quit comedy long before reaching the level of success required to be interviewed for a history book.

My gripe is not with the book itself. It feels like Horan and Matthews made every attempt to rectify any imbalance by making the definition of comedy wider than sketch and stand-up, by moving into the realms of writing, theatre and cabaret. In their search for interview subjects the authors have looked beyond the obvious, and the perspectives offered are multi-generational. The book feels optimistic and finishes on a high note, documenting Rose Matefeo's extraordinary success at the Edinburgh Fringe in 2018. There's a new crop of comedians coming through, and comedy is more diverse than ever.

At the time of writing, the impending sale of MediaWorks, including TV3, has been announced. It is too soon to know what the long-term effect on comedy will be, but, as this book shows, comedy is not about the method of delivery, or even about broadcast television. Formats will continue to change and there will always be a person wanting to make sense of the world, looking to connect with an audience and laugh together.

A High Point of Connectivity

by Peter Simpson

Peat by Lynn Jenner (Otago University Press, 2019), 274pp, $35

While reading Lynn's Jenner's engaging and idiosyncratic book *Peat*, I was reminded of a passage I encountered as a student. It was a definition by Samuel Johnson of Metaphysical wit as 'a kind of *discordia concors*; a combination of dissimilar images or discovery of occult resemblances in things apparently unlike ... The most heterogeneous ideas are yoked by violence together.' Johnson was being critical of a manner he disliked, but the best Metaphysical poetry of Donne and Herbert transcends his censure and so, on the whole, does Lynn Jenner's book-length demonstration of 'harmonious discord', in which she yokes together (with some violence) the heterogeneous subjects of the building of the Kāpiti Expressway in 2013–17 near her home in Raumati South with the life and career of Dunedin poet and editor Charles Brasch (1909–1973), 40 years dead at the time of the road's construction.

A collection of intermixed essays on the two subjects occupies the first half of the book, followed by two extensive glossaries: 'One Starless Night' dealing with Brasch (61 pages), and 'The Prettiest Road in New Zealand' dealing with the expressway (43 pages). Jenner is quite candid about her methodology, writing in an Author's Note: 'The framework of a glossary allowed me to explore the language of these two subjects and to record questions and reflections as I spoke to people, read books, newspapers and poems and formed my own ideas' (p. 8). In the first essay, 'A Necessary Protection', she further explains: 'As the Expressway showed itself, arriving like an army in each new location along the route, I knew I needed the close company of a writer as bulwark against all its enacted power and concrete. I needed to gather up pages and pages of words and take them inside with me, to a place where machines could not follow' (p. 9).

The choice of Brasch as a bulwark or antidote to the expressway with its political and industrial clamour and its in-your-face actuality was far from random. Brasch was simultaneously remote and connected; a male writer from another time and place, patrician in his privacy and reserve, but a man of words and books and, for Jenner, a refuge from the hard insistence of machinery, noise and associated partisan controversy. On the other hand, there was much to connect the author with Brasch. She, too, is a poet, who grew up in the same city, although 'your Dunedin and mine were very different', she comments (p. 11); she, too, is of Jewish lineage, though her parents' pharmacy was a world away from the wealth and cultivated opulence of Brasch's background of mercantile privilege. Nevertheless, Brasch, like her, was engaged in environmental, heritage and political conflicts of the time, as manifested, for instance, in his numerous letters to the *Otago Daily Times* or his editorial Notes for *Landfall*. Brasch even paid a visit to the Kāpiti Coast in 1950 (to call on Douglas Lilburn), describing the experience quite extensively in his journal, his account affording Jenner a high point of connectivity. Thus, there is a complex pattern of likeness and unlikeness which links Brasch to Jenner and vice versa.

In the chapters on Brasch, Jenner explores a variety of novel approaches to her subject. She begins by immersing herself in Brasch's library in Special Collections at Otago University, struck by the fact that it is a collection that 'goes everywhere' in terms of time, place and genre, and remarking: 'No house I have ever lived in could contain this many books'(p. 12). Jenner is especially interested in Brasch's family history which she explores largely through his posthumous autobiography, *Indirections* (1980), a book she describes in a chapter heading as 'Charles Brasch's [largely] Unloved Memoir'. She is especially fascinated by his grandfather, Willi Fels, and the central role he played in the development of Otago Museum, while recognising how dated and ethnocentric his cultural attitudes were. She visits Brasch's former house at 36a Heriot Row as it is undergoing an extensive make-over, noting that, '[w]indows influenced by the arts and crafts movement and a dwarf maple outside the front bedroom are the only signs that beauty mattered here' (p. 105). She engages in a couple of chapters of deft literary analysis, first of Brasch's late poem 'Clear', and then in a rich eleven-part discussion of the poem 'Lady Engine', fruitfully comparing it to a prose account of the same childhood dream in *Indirections*, which, putting on her hat as former psychologist, she interprets in the light of Brasch's painful loss of his mother Helene when he was only four.

These chapters on Brasch are interspersed with diverse takes on the construction of the expressway. Jenner starts with the geology of the environment over which the expressway is constructed, as presented in an information booth designed to inform the public via boxes of peat, sand (two types), gravel and rock, representing the successive layers of material laid down on the coastline. Other chapters explore such topics as the possible presence of a taniwha affected by the construction and what reality this might have for 'a Pākehā woman of Jewish and Celtic origin' (p. 19), and the open day that is held by the Alliance which built the expressway, in order that locals might walk along it before it opens to vehicles—an opportunity that the author takes up along with thousands of others. Although Jenner is generally anxious and troubled about the expressway development—for example, she speaks of it as 'an exoskeleton, expanding across the sand and the wetlands ... as if it was steel spreading across my own skin (p. 23)—she is admirably free from partisan zealotry, and genuinely tries to see all sides of the question. She writes, for example:

> Right from the beginning, in 2009, I had been unable to arrive at a simple 'love it or hate it' view of the expressway. My natural sympathy was more with the opponents of the Expressway, because, for environmental reasons, I wanted to see less emphasis on roads rather than more, but I saw, every day, that the version of Highway 1 that ran through Kāpiti was grossly unsafe and completely inadequate for the job. (p. 41)

This fair-minded and truth-seeking approach is evident throughout the most extensive essay, 'Sixteen Chapters of the Kāpiti Expressway Noise Story', an attempt to investigate from all sides the complexities of the post-construction noise problem for those living near the expressway and the various efforts to respond to the problem, constrain the protests about it and ameliorate it. The author attends meetings and briefings by experts and politicians, talks to affected residents and other interested parties, and even takes a leaf out of Brasch's book by writing letters to public officials. She is frustrated by the difficulty she finds in marshalling her arguments effectively, and humbled by the ineffectiveness of her attempts to intervene and make a difference. She is filled with renewed respect for the confidence and cogency of Brasch's advocacy for causes he believed in, such as landscape and building preservation and the promotion of architectural standards. Her honesty and refusal to simplify complex issues are impressive: 'Stories of the present resist endings. They are toddlers who won't go to bed. They wave their little white arms in front of your face and tell you that tomorrow will be even more interesting than today' (p. 148).

The two glossaries range from entries of a line or two to essays of several pages. Some entries are keyed by asterisks to details in the earlier essays; others stand alone. Inevitably, given the alphabetic arrangement, the material reaches the reader in random order, contributing to the general effect of 'discordia'. For instance, in the Brasch glossary the first entries are 'accent', 'acceptance', 'acclimatize', 'anti-Semitism', 'archives'. We learn that Brasch disliked the Kiwi accent and modelled his own speech on that of his Anglophile aunts; that because his grandfather 'accepted me, finally, as I was' (p. 152) he became the 'rock and centre' of his life ('Fels' means 'rock' in German). Brasch's father anglicised his name to Henry Brash to avoid the pervasive if not overt anti-Semitism in Dunedin; Brasch changed it back. Details like these—there are hundreds of them—add substantially to Jenner's (and our) understanding of Brasch as a person.

The other glossary is heterodox in the extreme but contains much material of interest. I particularly enjoyed the entry on Patricia Grace, who defeated compulsory acquisition of her land by having it recognised as a Māori reserve. She forced a change of route for the expressway though, to her chagrin, this meant that some other Māori lost *their* land.

Throughout this worthy and absorbing book Jenner, as a poet, foregrounds and celebrates words, as in this eloquent passage under 'language': 'I use a bastard language, where the past and the present, confidence and doubt, logic and intuition live as equals' (p. 239).

The Dangers of Certain Types of Silence

by Emma Gattey

Life on Volcanoes: Contemporary essays
edited by Janet McAllister (Beatnik Publishing, 2019), 119pp, $25

This slender volume of essays is an *objet d'art*; beautiful dye spillages in warm watercolours span the cover, spine and pages like pastel Rorschach blots, tugging at you for response, interpretation, emotion. *Life on Volcanoes* will tell you a lot—about the authors, about yourself, about the deliberate and accidental construction of the world—in under 120 pages. Five essays, five women. Disparate threads yoked together by a punchy commission from Janet McAllister: 'Write whatever non-fiction you like.' The result, as McAllister summarises it, is an empathy-expanding, enlightening collection.

It starts with mortal danger, in Tze Ming Mok's letter to a friend presumably interned in one of the 're-education' (read: concentration) camps for Uighur Muslims in Xinjiang Uighur Autonomous Region of the People's Republic of China (PRC). 'After a Long Silence' addresses a recipient with no known address, in a territory where human beings are 'disappeared' and friends are 'taken out like a virus'. Mok's writing is powerfully riverine, her prose propulsive, straining at the banks of thought and memory, pulling the reader in with the force of the Yangtze. Mok uses understatement and gentle, whispered truths that emerge through conversation with Han Chinese, sharing micro-histories, glimmers and experiences that rarely see the light of day within China, and which would need discreet word-of-mouth transmission or VPN protection to get out of the Middle Kingdom. These are stories to which few of us would be privy were it not for this missive.

Drawing links and firm dividing lines between peoples, groups and individuals, Mok introduces us to the popular metaphors of myrmecology. We learn that Han Chinese are known as 'Ants' in Xinjiang, viewed by persecuted Uighurs as a colonising force 'swarming into the city from the central provinces'. Extending the metaphor, Mok speaks of white settler colonialism in New Zealand and her own role 'as a part of that system, a worker in the Queen's colony'. She is excellent on the ways these armies of Ants are deployed by various arms of the Communist Party of China as well as New Zealand political parties. Musing on a global game of epic economic proportions (where the important players are nation-states and 'the house always wins'), Mok's diagnosis is grim: we face 'paralysing public silence from our leaders' over mounting PRC influence in New Zealand. Nor is Mok forgiving of her own silence. She regrets her inertia upon learning of the camps, and her terrified, wilful blindness regarding those 'places people enter, but which no-one leaves'.

Somehow, within the bleakness, Mok is terribly funny (see the almost slapstick recounting of her grandfather's defection from China). With undertones of Cold War espionage, she frequently refers to 'our mutual friend', some shady agent from a John Le Carré novel. But the anonymity here is not for literary effect. It is to protect her friends from the global reach of the Chinese panopticon. This essay is the work of a public intellectual, tinged with grief and remorse, playful in its black humour, intent on breaking this officially endorsed silence.

In 'A Bed of Volcanoes: Sex, fantasy, revolution', Tui Gordon traces a unique military history: the 'sex wars' between successive waves of feminism. Echoing Jessa Crispin's manifesto, *Why I Am Not a Feminist*, Gordon rails against the current omni-permissiveness of feminist thought. She denounces the toxic, hollowed-out 'You-Do-You' version of feminism, saying it is nothing more than an etiolated, theory-less justification for self-indulgence, hyper-consumerism and individualism, blind to intersectionality and inter-related forms of justice (social, economic, climate).

Gordon, too, is riotously funny, describing the cognitive dissonance baked into the word 'lesbian', which simultaneously conjures up 'two very antithetical things: a porn category and a pair of short-haired older women in matching anoraks and sensible sandals'. But she takes us beyond simple (false) binaries, explaining the nuanced chiaroscuro nature of sexuality, its intermingling of pleasure, pain, vulnerability and power, and what she once saw as the fundamental revolutionary potential of sex. Fluidly blending analysis of queer sexual repression, rape fantasies and the catharsis of Disney's *Moana*, Gordon shares her struggle to 'exercise the elusive art of self-care', which is essential to maintaining the stamina and compassion required to support someone battling with trauma. In a beautiful Anne Salmond-inspired register, Gordon turns towards mātauranga Māori for answers, for healing, for help. She learns that emotional resilience can come through nurturing an emotional connection to the earth, and makes the 'mind-bending, inter-language' discovery that in te reo, the senses (rongo) include sensing things with your ngākau (heart-energy) and wairua (spirit energy). 'Whakarongo' therefore means not merely to listen, but 'to actively receive all kinds of sensory and energetic impulses'. So, Gordon concludes, we ought to expand our sensory and compassion registers, our very ways of being in the world.

Tulia Thompson's 'In the Under: Being poor and dreaming the end of capitalism' is a personal phenomenology of poverty and precarity in Aotearoa, demanding that we acknowledge 'the failure of neoliberal capitalism'. Echoing Christine Dann's *Up From Under*, Thompson's version of 'the Under' is a literary loan-word from New Zealand novelist Anna Smaill, adapted to mean 'short of money, and in a changed, bleak emotional landscape'. Although she tries to see a latent kinetic energy in the 'Under', the possibility of 'agency in actively seeking out ways to stay afloat', Thompson comes to realise the falsity of this agency. Financial precarity is isolating and debasing in its frenetic stasis: the need to keep frantically moving just to stay in one place, treading water in the stagnant pond of your own life.

Thompson explores the demeaning taxonomy of poverty, the intoxicating rags-to-riches progress narrative ('You can put up with a lot of shit if you're convinced that things are going to get better'), the oppressive racial exceptionalism of Pākehā education systems, and offers an anti-capitalist reading of Mansfield, Ihimaera, Smaill and Dickens. The writing doesn't always cohere, and her literary referents seem cherry-picked and ill-matched, but her analysis is interesting. In the highlight of the piece, Thompson uses 'five silences' to trace the nexus between global capitalism and Aotearoa's 'current capitalist moment', the ideology baked into the structures of our society. Ranging from the profoundly personal to the national, each silence reveals deliberate decisions, premised on the global capitalist 'logic' that 'protection of capital is more important than alleviating human suffering'. This gossamer thread connects Mok and Thompson's writings: the intersection between individual lives and realpolitik, the official silence on documented human rights abuses abroad. Under our global and domestic systems, individual lives are inferior to the greasing of global supply chains. None of this is allegory. Nor is it beautiful, ornate writing. But it is courageous. It is blunt, matter-of-fact personal history. And in its realism, in its determined humourlessness, it mirrors the relentless grind of the Under.

While Mok, Gordon and Thompson explore asymmetries of power and ways to heal the resulting imbalances, Courtney Sina Meredith focuses on a completely different, deeply intimate kind of healing. Meredith's '107 Years' refers to the cumulative years of 'excessive bleeding and chronic pain' endured by five women in her family. Tracing the whakapapa of chronic pain ('a dowry centuries old'), Meredith describes women bound together by ribbons of blood and suffering, her own diagnosis of endometriosis and hormonal imbalance, and her reclamation of her body through radical self-love. Of course, it starts with a poem. Of course, it is harrowing, beautiful, honest. Although Meredith writes of the pain preventing her from 'living [her] best life', she still falls in love, writes prolifically, secures an audience for her voice. The spectral genius of Katherine Mansfield haunts Meredith's acknowledgement that ceaseless pain and fatigue 'became *meaningful* ... a source to draw from and create'. In sharp contrast to the alienation recounted by Thompson, Meredith realises the 'golden thread of [her] mahi': her focus on her work was a panacea, if not literally anaesthetic; it saved her life, kept her going, even spurred creativity.

Finally, Ruth Larsen's 'December Smells Like Hairspray' is a rollicking ride through the insecurities, aerosol and coping mechanisms that are part of parenthood—specifically, 'the matrix of children's activities'. Larsen takes us through a mindboggling ('undeniably gendered') vortex of expensive and time-consuming hobbies, life-skills and extra-curriculars. This vortex depicts the deeply structured time of childhood, the pressure of perpetual advancement and of 'stacking units' of extra-curriculars, of upgrading your children, readying them for life, the workplace, for the market—a pressure that seems to be intensifying generationally. Year by year, term by term, day by day, Gen Z children face a war of attrition against leisure. In the false (but socially accepted) calculus of our time, the opportunity cost of play is self-enhancement, self-marketability, opportunities which another parent is surely seizing for their own child. This is what Larsen labels the 'middle-class shuffle', a harried state of status-anxiety where parents raise their children to be prize pigs on the job market, the most appealing candidates with the plumpest of resumés, the thickest set of qualifications.

Combining wildly different experiences of life in Aotearoa and the wider world, this brilliant collection of essays is woven through with shared concerns of climate crisis and anxiety, alienation, self-care and self-critique, concealments (pain, motives, fear), and the dangers of certain types of silence.

A Longing for Association and Closeness

by John Geraets

Verses by Lola Ridge (Quale Press, 2019), 176pp., $US18; **Two Or More Islands** by Diana Bridge (Otago University Press, 2019), 88pp., $27.95; **The Dangerous Country of Love and Marriage** by Amy Leigh Wicks (Auckland University Press, 2019), 88pp., $24.99

Like so many other things, a risk that poetry seems to face nowadays is that it works like a lolly scramble. All are welcome to participate and everyone leaves with a sweet in their pocket. Given this 'something-for-everyone' syndrome, how should one compose a very brief review of three considerable publications by three individual women who represent more than three generations of poetry writing? How balance appreciation, discernment and a sense of connection? Well, I can say at the outset that there are very good things to be said about each of these books, just as there are also some reservations that can be expressed.

Lola Ridge's *Verses*, described by editor Michele Leggott as 'a textual Google Earth for its day', derives from a manuscript submitted in the early 1900s to the *Sydney Bulletin*. The poems, conventional in form and content, are presented as 'precursors' (formative work) to the mature poetry of 'American Modernist Lola Ridge'. Our second book, *Two Or More Islands* by Diana Bridge, is rightly considered an 'indigenous' and contemporary book (the poet's seventh), though a major portion of the poems are actually located in other terrains and are concerned with the thought of other worlds, Asian and Greek. Our third book, *The Dangerous Country of Love and Marriage*, evoking thoughts of Chaucer's ageless 'To speke of wo that is in mariage', is by the 'twenty-nine years old' New York poet Amy Leigh Wicks. Her poems are autobiographical and trace a journey from a difficult New York childhood, through her meeting and absconding on a road trip with her prospective husband, Matthew, a decision to sell their motorcycles in favour of plane tickets to Wellington, and her subsequent enrolment at the International Institute of Modern Letters at Victoria University, an influence reflected in the poems.

Fair to say that the three books stretch our thinking on time and New Zealandness. In terms of their personal compass, being female, the literary culture, social attitudes, their sense of personal utterance and public disclosure, each is distinctly individual. And allowing for the fact that, in our globalised world, such a reaching across geographies and timelines is of no great matter, I will take these writers in reverse order and focus on their use of poetic language in exploring their life circumstances.

Of the three I find *Dangerous Country* the most fresh and captivating. It charms the reader because, while the revelations are candid, the voice in the poems resonates with a vulnerability that doesn't collapse into either self-justification or complaint. The emotional confidences, balancing disappointment with anticipation, include wit and humour. Writing is the chance to self-renovate:

> There I am, curled up like a child crying out
> all of my fears. Here I am, wiping my eyes
> to read each word as it is written
> ('Rapha')

> it was just me, alone with the bruise
> of a bad decade, finally asking toward the sky
> for a little help, shuddering ugly tears until
> I was dry in the silence of an answer I'm still
> learning to understand.
> ('Epiphany')

The astute phrasing matches the shifting ratios of the emotions recounted. Likewise, the images, poised and concise (one is reminded of Sylvia Plath), hinge between pain and the prospect of renascence:

> I woke twenty years later
> writing these poems
> ('Remnant')

> I married a man on a motorcycle from out
> west
> and left my city, my state, my country for love
> ('Landing')

> until finally, a new thing can grow.
> ('Everything Ruined')

One reservation I have is that, through the course of the books as the poet adapts to physical New Zealand and a more 'homely' emotional and social environment, the self-revelatory tautness of the poems seems to relax and the voice becomes more discursive. What will happen as this engaging young poet navigates a way beyond a poetic devoted to personal utterance (for example, the early sonnet 'Bildungsroman' contains no less than 14 variants of the 'I' pronoun, only one 'you', one 'we' and four 'its')? How might this work evolve beyond a reliance on empathic affiliation, as I expect it must and will?

Diana Bridge writes within a more cerebral tradition. Wit, syllogism, learnedness—the disclosures are a result of an adroit rumination rather than of any 'spontaneous overflow of powerful feelings'. The poems, fifteen of the forty-eight actually carrying explanatory footnotes, are based on travels in Asia and forays into Asian and Greek literature and mysticism. The poet sets out to elucidate deeply embedded patterns:

> To unroll symbol and to weave connection,
> the lines and trigrams, and the trigrams
> doubled,
> Must be yoked to words.
> ('Encountering *The Book of Change*')

What particularly interests me, in contrast to the more effusive Amy Leigh Wicks, is the degree of emotional reserve that is built into these poems. It is a quality that is impressive and will undoubtedly appeal to many readers, although to my own mind there is a tendency for the poems to become caught up in intellectual discriminations that at times results in a clotted use of language. The italicised words (my addition) in the opening poem, 'Re-visiting the Magnolia', show this 'heady' aspect:

> Last year it offered like a *sacrament* its
> *complement*
> of cups. Now, *chalices* the colour of *communion*
> *wafers* have *loosened* to let in the *shocking* red
> of stamens, and boughs *lack all rapport*

We are ushered into a sacerdotal world in which the extended simile risks overwhelming the poor tree, to the extent that the 'boughs lack all rapport'. Otherwise, the combination of decorous use of language and the exotic allusions is generally skilfully managed, and deserves appreciation. The message is that profundities (revelations, treasures), promised through spiritual thought and discoverable within one's own experience, need to be extracted:

> Words start in an underworld, its byways
> ready to be mined.
> ('J.H. Prynne in China')

Related to this unearthing enterprise, the poems repeatedly warn against the attendant hazards: false allures, entrapment, the ordure of extraction, the failed quest for release (see: 'Was There Ever an Avernus?', 'Add a Name Like Sappho').

More immediate and heartfelt poems include the unusually grim 'Brothers' and the charming 'Dream Analogue':

> It is her daughter who holds onto me;
> as we cross she clings like a koala to my
> back.

'Mine Eyes Dazzle' achieves something similar:

> Then I, my darling, for the first time in years,
> took my eyes off your face and started seeing
> reasons.

This quintessential poem proclaims Bridge's endeavour

> to push aside the red-gold patterns of the
> surface
> in search of underpinnings, the foundation,
> any base.

However, the implication is that no such 'foundation' likely exists ('There is never a base') and, in the end, it is only within the quest itself that illumination resides.

While it is gratifying to have substantial poets like Lola Ridge brought into the New Zealand literary context, it also reveals a predicament for us. What identifies a poet with a country, and how are we to discriminate between various parts of a poet's oeuvre, especially when as in this case the links are tenuous? Arguably, the main achievement (and it is considerable!) of the book is that of scholar-editor-poet Leggott. The scholarship is meticulous; and what it inadvertently highlights is that this early work of Ridge, who was to become an 'anarcho-feminist' activist and noted Modernist poet in the USA through the late 1910s and 1920s, is intrinsically without great distinction. Ridge, Irish-born in 1873, spent much of her early life in New Zealand (arriving around 1880), before returning to Sydney in 1903 and from there moving in 1907 to settle permanently in the USA, where she reached poetry maturity before slipping again into obscurity in the 1930s. The predicament (drawback) is that the valuation process has occurred in retrospect rather than in prospect, as Leggott is inclined to argue: 'This investigation sets out to find the antipodean poet Lola Ridge and to connect her with the American Modernist Lola Ridge.' It is hard to make the connection between the clear-eyed Modernist Ridge and this earlier Romantic one:

> Beneath the flutter of the rising stars,
> Beyond the ratas where the red sun dips
> Are bays & galaxies of fair white ships;
> A dull surf booms upon the distant bars—
> ('At Sun-Down')

'Flutter, dips, red, fair, white, dull, booms' are examples of weak descriptors, despite the local references ('rātā' is listed six times in the glossary, of 46 poem entries).

This is not to suggest that *Verses* is inferior to other local work of its own era. There is a sense of energy, exploration, openness, vivacity, determination, celebration, personal anguish, an 'Australasian' temperament, and a longing for association and closeness, as the following extract might indicate:

> Now is no need to serve
> Or suffer or regret: it seems life holds
> No future & no past for me but this
> Sun-lighted mountain & the brooding bush.
> ('Lake Kanieri')

Another reflection of the somewhat uphill endeavour to grant a special legitimacy to Ridge's early work is that, in her lengthy Introduction, Leggott spends several pages discussing the considerably higher achievement of the poet's subsequent work in the key 1920 volume, *Sun-Up and Other Poems*, in particular the title piece. While Leggott speaks of a 'continuum' ('one version of the events and another', 'shuttle back and forth'), at least for me the overall impression is that the early poems come across as a derivative of the later, more accomplished work, on which their value depends.

This first and final book to be considered deserves commendation insofar as it continues to broaden the accumulating literary archive and the remarkable literary scholarship we have available, as it also brings to light work that has tended to be neglected (or disparaged) on the presumption that it is merely either feminine or colonialist or both.

Charting the Past

Mairéad de Róiste

Singing the Trail: The story of mapping Aotearoa New Zealand by John McCrystal (Allen & Unwin, 2019), 276pp., $59.99

Maps are evocative. Roads to travel, places to see, locations to experience. They forge a connection with a landscape often outside our here and now. John McCrystal's *Singing the Trail: The story of mapping Aotearoa New Zealand* is one of two cartographic atlases published in New Zealand last year and provides a beautiful retrospective of historical interpretations of New Zealand. Given the history of cartography, unsurprisingly the book primarily has a Western or colonial lens. McCrystal charts a path through twelve themes to discuss the expansion of cartographic knowledge of New Zealand. His accompanying text is informative and occasionally irreverent.

Singing the Trail opens with McCrystal's personal reflections on the influence of maps, navigation and place-making. Maps are the stories we tell of place. They are cartographic depictions of landscape, but they are not the only ways of describing the land, and were certainly not the first. McCrystal acknowledges the place of oral maps, highlighting the role of waiata, karakia, myths and legends as methods of learning and communicating geographic knowledge. The exploration of the seas around Aotearoa by Polynesian seafarers and European navigators before the existence of physical maps engenders a sense of wonder.

As we move through McCrystal's chapters, blank spaces are filled and the maps begin to resemble our known world. New Zealand takes shape in increasing detail. One of the interesting strands within the atlas is the early tracing of imaginary lands mistakenly placed on the world map, and how these appeared or disappeared from cartographic knowledge.

We learn more about the mapmakers and the impact of their experience and knowledge on the geographic view of the world. One enduring impact of early maps, particularly those made by James Cook, can be seen in the place names dotted around current maps of Aotearoa. As Tipene O'Regan says, place names are the 'survey pegs of memory'. Externally imposed place names record a mapmaker's memories and often override other concepts of places, in particular, Māori names and significance.

The late eighteenth- and early nineteenth-century charting of New Zealand's coastline by whalers and sealers seeking to exploit local resources offers a glimpse into a lost world, and only hints at the journeys the mapmakers undertook and the impact on iwi ('here we took on board a native'). The effort required to create these maps can scarcely be imagined; the resultant impact on wildlife has been well documented elsewhere. The atlas also portends the devasting navigational impacts—mis-charted courses and shipwrecks—of geographic information that was not shared.

McCrystal acknowledges that the settlement of New Zealand by the British came at a harsh cost for Māori, who increasingly recognised that the depiction of land on maps was not often cause for celebration. Like history, maps record particular perspectives. As a reader, I experienced a growing sense of dread as the maps evolved to show colonial settlements enclosing and overwriting Māori communities, as spaces were claimed and became divorced from their history and geography. The imposition of rigid order on a landscape sacrifices a connection with topography—rivers, mountains, bays—in favour of straight lines and grids.

Singing the Trail communicates the excitement of the discovery of new places and the joy of exploration. McCrystal is more forgiving of the impact of mapmakers who explore and 'discover' than of those who survey known areas. Maps are not simple statements of fact or geography: they are a product of their time and author. The same can be said for this compendium. The book is not a critical reading of New Zealand's mapping history and impacts; it allows readers to draw their own conclusions about the 'discovery' and mapping of places that were already known and understood by their inhabitants.

The theme-driven collation seems forced at times. Some earlier chapters provide a single-minded approach to a multi-faceted representation of the landscape, where the historical narrative competes with the thematic divisions. The introduction of Stokes and Drury's 1858 map illustrating the contemporary knowledge of New Zealand's coastline lacks the important context, provided later in the book, of the iwi rōpū prominently displayed on the map. As well, there is an expectation throughout that readers are familiar with the geography of New Zealand; a map compendium referencing locations mentioned would have been worthwhile.

McCrystal's decision to move away from the historical or chronological inclusion of maps in the later chapters is supported. Chapter 10 'Places in the Heart' depicts military engagements in Le Quesnoy, Gallipoli and East Jordan, and war graves in Crete, and makes sombre reading. Chapter 11 'A Moving Story' charts the transition from sea travel to road, rail and air networks, and illustrates the impact on the countryside of changing modes of transport.

Singing the Trail allows us to trace the stories of familiar places. The discovery of the origins of the railway from Wellington allowed me to revisit the landscape anew. Taken together, the maps explain seemingly random human-made features and enable a deeper understanding of where we are.

Aesthetically, the maps and charts are a delight, though the resolution of some may leave the reader wanting more. While McCrystal doesn't expound on cartographic techniques, the sheer variety of mapping in the atlas indulges the reader to explore different symbols and methods of representation. Historic maps often trade the accuracy and urgency of digital navigation for more engaging imaginings of space and place-making. The hachures of Stokes' Chart of the Cook Strait evoke a landscape ripe for the imagination. I was particularly delighted to see the inclusion of Koch's lighthouse map (1900), which provides a pleasing example of decorative but informative symbology and insight into a time when sea navigation still played a fundamental role in the making of places.

The atlas leaves us with a sense of the here and now, ending (somewhat abruptly) with a satellite image of New Zealand showing the country in true colour amid cloud patterns. This verdant landscape is our final view. We know that human habitation has had a dramatic impact on vegetation cover, but strangely, other human impacts on the landscape—routes, cities and other settlements—are difficult to discern. This image is also divorced from our personal experiences of the landscape. Perhaps this map strikes the right balance by representing the current mapmaking age of greater detail, more accurate and timely methods, fewer unknowns, but with a loss of aesthetics and the joy of discovery, sense-making and connection to place.

The 276-page hard-cover edition is a welcome volume for both map geeks and general readers interested in cartography or hydrography.

The Unseen Moment

by David Eggleton

The New Photography: New Zealand's first-generation contemporary photographers by Athol McCredie (Te Papa Press, 2019), 216pp., $70

'Talk to photographers and you are quickly caught by a new excitement in New Zealand photography. They look at the world as rhythms of light—a jam session, peaking all over the place, and if they are ready then—*click*, it can be captured ... Photography now is a movement.' Thus, Geoff Chapple, writing in the *NZ Listener* in 1976 and quoted by Athol McCredie in his Introduction to *The New Photography*, an anthology of photography portfolios and interviews with photographers.

By 1976 the 'new photography'—which McCredie also refers to as 'contemporary photography', but which is perhaps better termed 'street photography'—had become established as a dominant idiom in New Zealand photography, its influence felt in photojournalism and advertising as well as in photographic exhibitions and publications.

The idea that photography could be 'art' had been fostered by camera clubs and societies in New Zealand since the end of the nineteenth century, but only gradually, with the arrival of Modernist ideas in the mid-twentieth century, did 'art photography' stop slavishly imitating fine art painting and become what McCredie terms 'thinking photography ... self-aware photography ... attentive to ephemeral moments and surreal juxtapositions [seen] through an antipodean filter'.

The selections in *The New Photography* end more or less in 1976 with the mainstream acknowledgement of 'street photography' and begin ten years earlier, more or less, when street photography was just beginning to take off in this country as an avant-garde phenomenon—but as ever in a medium as quicksilver, elusive and as ubiquitous as photography, the story is complicated. McCredie attempts to simplify it by making his book a strategic and limited survey of the work of just eight photographers—Gary Baigent, Richard Collins, John Daley, John Fields, Max Oettli, John B. Turner, Len Westney and Ans Westra—while omitting a number of other significant figures.

The 1960s are legendary as a time of credos and manifestos. An atmosphere of cultural and social change, a radical eagerness, was in the air. The New Photographers arose out of this milieu. Ans Westra was already well known by the mid-1960s for her photographs in various government propaganda-style publications that emphasised harmonious assimilation, but she saw with an unblinkered eye. This Dutch migrant early on brought a Europe-trained artistic sensibility to bear on depictions of embryonic identity politics, on biculturalism, feminism, consumerism. In this she anticipated the cultural transformations of the 1970s and 1980s. Her images, as McCredie's selection reveals, offer parables and allegories for the human condition, and these in turn owe their initial impetus to Edward Steichen's famous 1950s photographic exhibition *The Family of Man*, which Westra saw as a teenager in Amsterdam: 'I bought the catalogue and lived with it and loved its concept of pictures and quotes.'

John Fields was another migrant photographer. An American, he arrived in New Zealand in 1966, recruited to work as a specialist science photographer at the University of Auckland. Like Westra, he brought an outsider's eye to bear on a small insular nation at a time of transition. Familiar with American Transcendentalism, with the writings of Thoreau and Emerson, Fields' fine-grained, luminously beautiful images often reveal a near religious feel for the aura of objects. They suggest a hallowing of the everyday, as in his image of daylight reflected from the sea's surface at Waiheke Island, or in the image of a sleeping baby cocooned under a transparent rainhood in a pushchair. For this poet of the lens, each photograph a sermon with a camera, another vital subject was the entropic colonial city, where derelict buildings were being torn down for a motorway. There's an end-of-Empire elegiac air to these images with their meditative depictions of architecture at the moment of exhaustion, this vacancy a prelude to demolition.

Technically proficient, Fields shared his photographic darkroom skills with local photographers asserting the credo of Ansel Adams: 'the negative is the score, the print is the performance'.

Another evangelist for the careful crafting of the Modernist photograph was John B. Turner, the single most influential workshop teacher of the time and in charge of the photography department at Elam Art School. Turner's own photographs extol proletarian virtues. He photographs men energetically pushing wheelbarrows around a building site, a helpful NZ Railways ticket collector, and train passengers gently snoozing.

For other photographers the camera is a device for self-declaration. McCredie makes much of Gary Baigent's *The Unseen City: 123 photographs of Auckland*, published in 1967 by Blackwood and Janet Paul. Printed in an edition of 5000 on cheap uncoated paper that flattened contrast and suppressed detail, Baigent's photo-book, 'rough as guts', was considered shocking by photography purists. Yet, electric, kinetic, insouciant, each photograph looking as granular as matter itself, Baigent's sequence of images heralds a new vitality, a new sensibility: one that was gritty, fresh, immediate, intimate. As Baigent recalls here, 'I wanted to grab an image of life that was natural.' Influenced by French New Wave cinema as much as photographs seen in overseas magazines such as *Look* and *Life*, Baigent stalks inner-city Auckland as if it's a mysterious labyrinth and he's a camera-slinger with sharp reflexes shooting from the hip, or a thief seizing the fleeting light and trapping it in a dark box, releasing it to flutter away like the pigeon over the Parnell railway freight yards on the cover of *The Unseen City*. His murky, phantom city is carnivalesque, cartoonish, covered in a patina of grease, oil and petrol.

Baigent's images possess an irreverent drollness; they represent the effervescence of the emergent youth culture, sounding the clarion call like a revved up internal combustion engine. And if Baigent leads the way, Richard Collins, John Daley and Max Oettli quickly follow. Their black and white photographs celebrate speed, restlessness and existential freewheeling. As Collins puts it in his interview, 'It all seemed to centre around the Kiwi Hotel, with parties and amazing conversations and introductions to other areas in arts and music ... we felt as though we could invent our own future.'

And so these photographs chronicle the lives of good keen blokes, hang-on-a-minute mates and milkbar cowboys zooming off on British motorbikes with female pillion passengers clinging on. The city, meanwhile, its roads, pavements and walls gored, scarred and greasy, has a topographical obliquity: you cannot identify actual places, only sensations are palpable.

A photograph by Richard Collins offers the bulging contours of an old-fashioned V8 muscle car, which rhyme with the bulging forearm of the driver propped on the car's open window. Entitled 'Auckland, 1967' the clinching detail is a bristling aggressive whip-like metal radio aerial that juts up and out of frame. The sound track to such photographs is rebellious rock music, the thudding drums, say, of Led Zeppelin, a band whose poster decorates an otherwise stark bedroom wall in an adjacent image by Gary Baigent.

Another Collins photograph suggests something more spiritual or blissful, offering the purity of white sand dunes, mānuka scrub, toetoe plumes and fleecy white cloud. The photograph seems to glisten, as though registering the breathing pores of the moment. The moment, though, has vanished, leaving behind the idyllic, hedonistic, sensuous surfaces of sand and seawater and bathers just out of sight, who come into frame in another photograph.

If Collins is a connoisseur of transitory beauty, Max Oettli is the photographer as urban flâneur, pursuing chance encounters like an entomologist with a butterfly net. He captures department-store shoppers with averted gazes crammed into a lift whose doors suddenly open; the lone diner in a coffee bar in a shaft of sunlight being peered at through the smeary plate glass by a gaggle of passers-by. Max Oettli's visual testimonies are full of humour as well as tenderness, but then in most of the images in this anthology good humour, affectionate and laconic, is never far away.

There's the disembodied giant hand protruding from a hedge in Len Westney's 'Plaster hand, children's play centre, Christchurch' (1972), and then there's his image of a bridal veil floating like angel wings, while a vicar's white vestment inflates like a life raft in the gusts of a hot Canterbury nor'wester in a church entranceway. For these photographers, it's all about the thrill of the chase, the securing of a clinching image, the capturing of an epiphany: the rush of the now that was then.

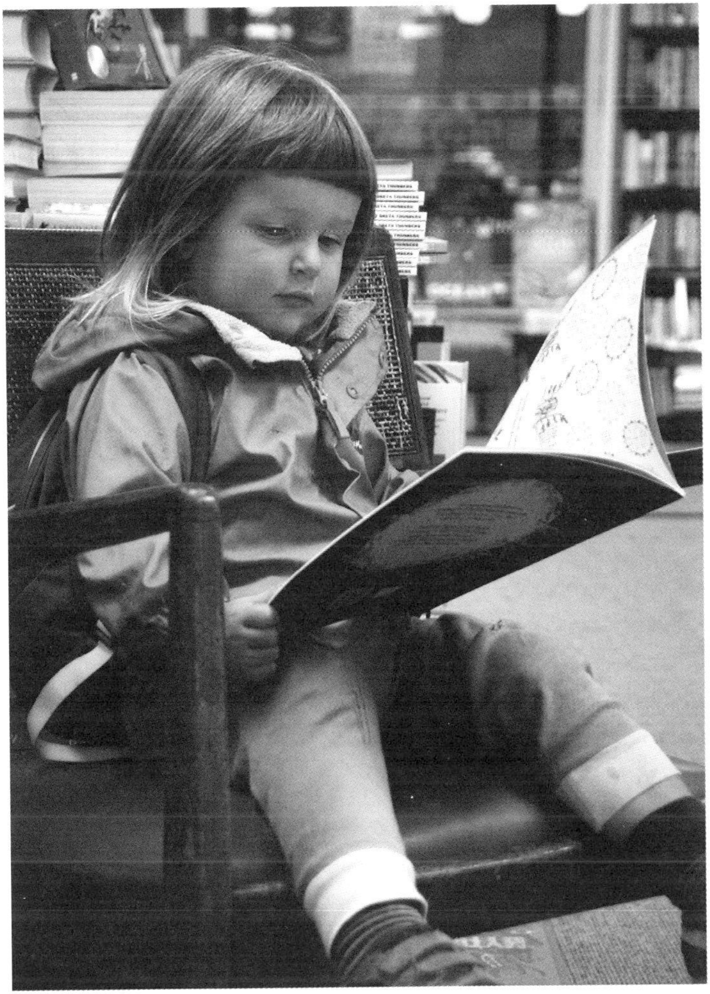

Victoria University Press
new fiction 2020

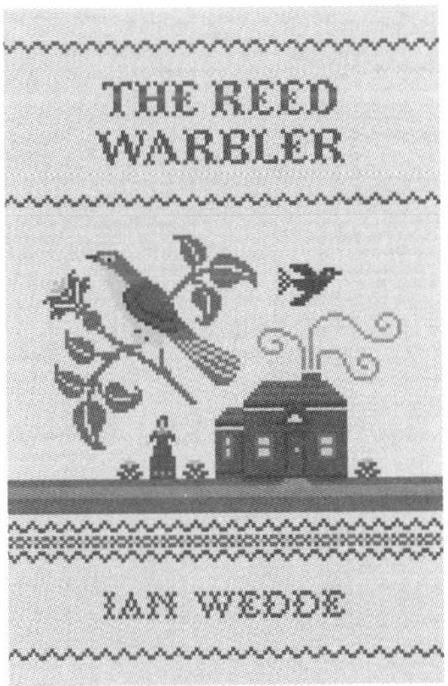

May, p/b, $35

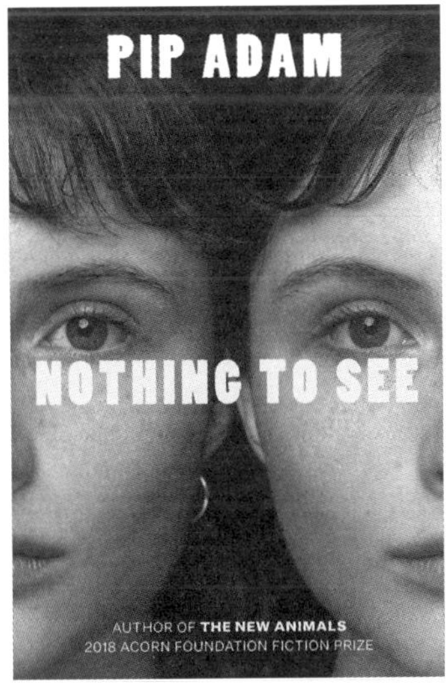

June, p/b, $30

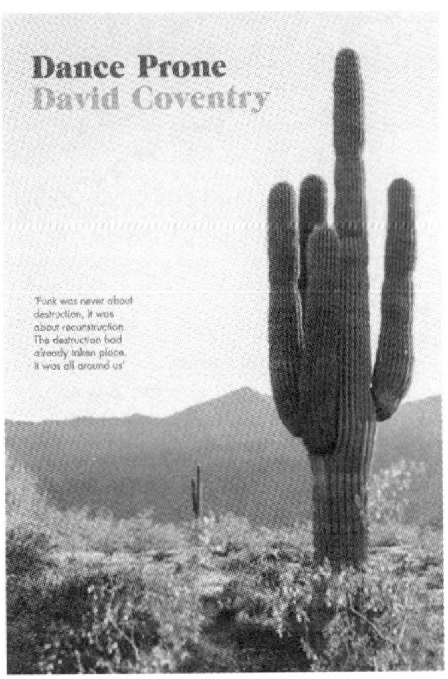

July, p/b, $35

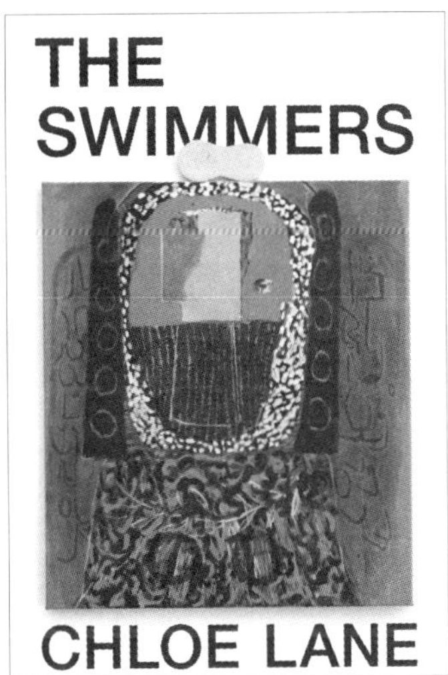

August, p/b, $30

NEW BOOKS FROM OTAGO

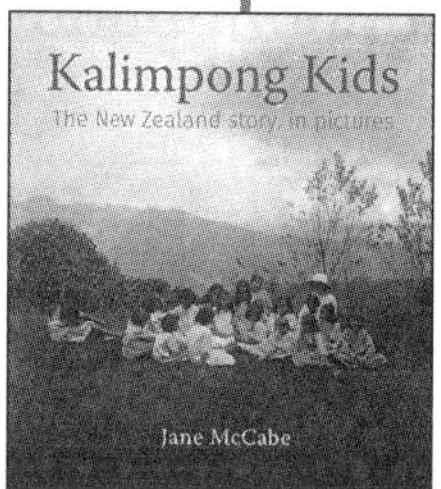

KALIMPONG KIDS: THE NEW ZEALAND STORY, IN PICTURES
JANE McCABE

In the early 20th century, 130 young Anglo-Indians were sent to New Zealand in an immigration scheme from Kalimpong, in the Darjeeling district of India. They were the children of British tea planters and local women, and were placed as workers with New Zealand families. Here is the compelling story, in pictures.

ISBN 978-1-98-859236-7, paperback, $35

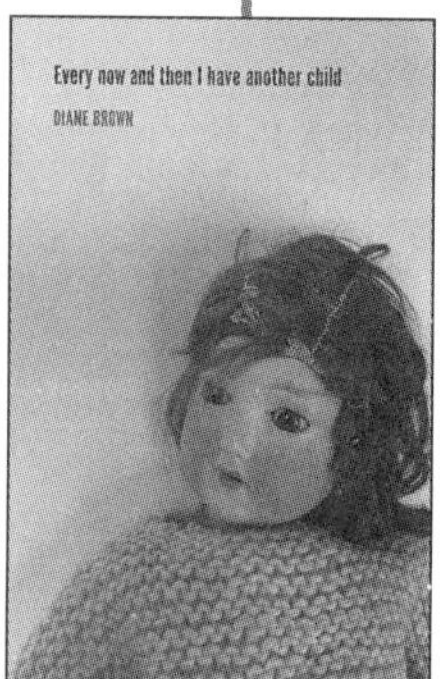

EVERY NOW AND THEN I HAVE ANOTHER CHILD
DIANE BROWN

A mysterious doppelgänger sister, a newborn baby, a boy in a mural, a detective, a former lover, a student stalker ... are they real or imagined? Building on Diane Brown's tradition of extended poetic narratives, this is an inventive and heartfelt meditation on motherhood, the creative impulse and the blurred line between imagination and reality.

ISBN 978-1-98-859240-4, paperback, $29.95

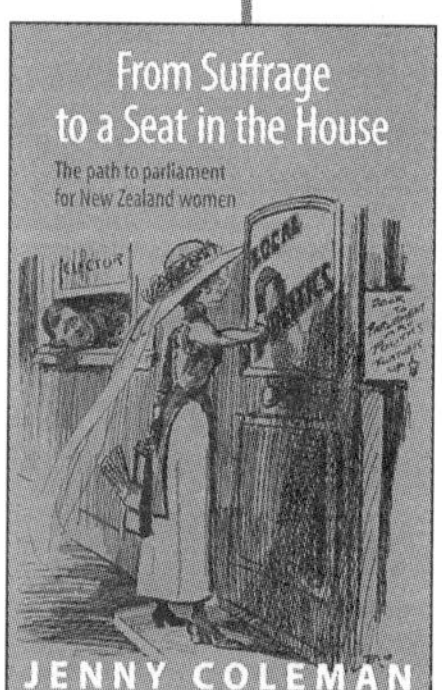

FROM SUFFRAGE TO A SEAT IN THE HOUSE: THE PATH TO PARLIAMENT FOR NEW ZEALAND WOMEN
JENNY COLEMAN

New Zealand has always proudly worn its status of being the first country to enfranchise women. But not many know that it took a further 40 long years to get the first woman elected to Parliament. The history of women striving to share in governing the country, a neglected footnote in the nation's electoral history, is now captured in this essential work by Jenny Coleman.

ISBN 978-1-98-859226-8, paperback, $45

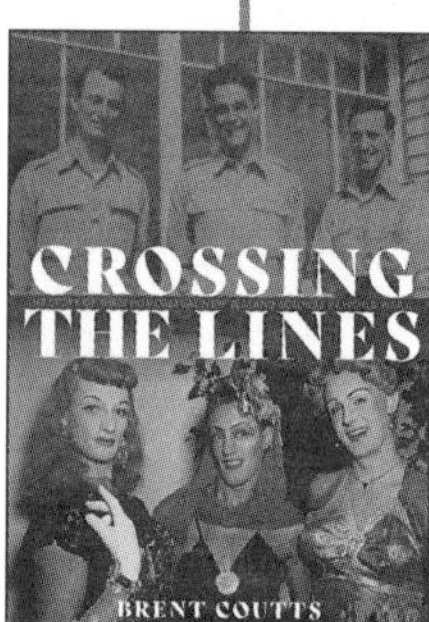

CROSSING THE LINES: THE STORY OF THREE HOMOSEXUAL NEW ZEALAND SOLDIERS IN WWII
BRENT COUTTS

Brent Coutts brings to light the previously untold history of New Zealand homosexual soldiers in World War II, drawing on the experiences of ordinary men who lived through extraordinary times. This is a story of strong friendships, the search for love and belonging as homosexuals within the military and civilian worlds, and the creation of the foundation of the queer community today.

ISBN 978-1-98-859238-1, paperback, $49.95

OTAGO UNIVERSITY PRESS
From good booksellers or www.otago.ac.nz/press

CONTRIBUTORS

John Adams is completing a PhD on Joan Retallack's experimental poetry at the University of Auckland, where he obtained a master's in creative writing in 2010. His collection *Briefcase* (Auckland University Press, 2011) won the Jessie Mackay Prize, and *Rumpelstiltskin Blues* (Steele Roberts, 2017) followed.

Johanna Aitchison is a Massey University PhD candidate. She was the 2019 Mark Strand Scholar at the Sewanee Writers' Conference, and her poem 'Buffalo' was published in *The Best Small Fictions: 2019 anthology* (Sonder Press).

John Allison has had poems published in many literary journals in NZ and overseas. His fifth collection of poetry, *A Place to Return To*, was published by Cold Hub Press in 2019.

Shaun Bamber is a proudly Pākehā-Māori farmer's son from Kaitāia. Educated at Waikato University and nearby Hillcrest Tavern, he has worked for the NZ railways, London-based homeless charity Shelter, *TV Guide*, Stuff and *Cook Islands News*. Now serving coffee and coconuts in Rarotonga with his wife and three kids.

Tony Beyer lives in Taranaki. His recent publications include 'Sand Fire', a long poem appearing online as *Mudlark Chap No. 67* and in print as *Friday Prayers* (Cold Hub Press, 2019).

Iain Britton is the author of several collections of poetry published in the UK and NZ. His poems have been published or are forthcoming in *Harvard Review*, *Poetry* (Chicago), the *New York Times*, *Stand*, *Agenda*, *New Humanist* and *Wild Court*. *The Intaglio Poems* was published by Hesterglock Press, UK, in 2017.

Medb Charleton divides her time between Ireland and NZ. She has a master's in creative writing from the IIML at Victoria University of Wellington and has recently contributed to nzpoetryshelf.com

Vita Cochran is a textile artist from Aotearoa who lives in Sydney. Her work, which engages with the histories of domestic craft, decoration and the work of women modernists, is held in the collections of Te Papa Tongarewa, Tāmaki Paenga Hira Auckland War Memorial Museum, the Dowse and many private collections. She has recently exhibited a series of hooked rugs called 'After Paintings', based on rugs that appear in modernist paintings. Vita is represented by Anna Miles Gallery in Auckland.

Ruth Corkill is a graduate of the Iowa Writers Workshop MFA programme. Her poetry has appeared in *The Feminist Wire*, *Landfall*, *NZ Listener*, *Poetry NZ*, *New Welsh Review*, *Wasafiri* and *The Moth*. She is pursuing a PhD in physics at the University of Stuttgart and was part of a Modern Languages Association symposium panel on Contemporary Physics Poetry.

Mairéad de Róiste is a senior lecturer in the School of Geography, Environment and Earth Sciences, Victoria University of Wellington. Originally from Ireland, she moved to NZ in 2006. She is interested in understanding how people use geographic information, and researches geospatial capability. She teaches cartography, geovisualisation and Geographic Information Science, and is an avid map reader.

Doc Drumheller was born in South Carolina and has lived in NZ for more than half his life. He has worked in award-winning groups for theatre and music and has published 10 collections of poetry. His poems have been translated into more than 20 languages. He lives in Oxford, where he edits and publishes the literary journal *Catalyst*.

Mark Edgecombe is a teacher, husband and father and lives and works in Tawa, north of Wellington.

Lynley Edmeades' second poetry collection, *Listening In*, was published in 2019 by Otago University Press. She lives in Dunedin with her partner and son.

David Eggleton is a poet, writer and critic who lives in Dunedin. His most recent collection of poems is *Edgeland and Other Poems* (Otago University Press, 2018). In 2019 he was appointed the New Zealand Poet Laureate, a title he will hold until 2021.

Johanna Emeney is a senior tutor in creative writing at Massey University, where she has worked for nine years. She also leads community writing projects with Ros Ali. Jo has published two collections of poetry (*Apple & Tree*, Cape Catley, 2011, and *Family History*, Mākaro Press, 2017), as well as an academic book: *The Rise of Autobiographical Medical Poetry and the Medical Humanities* (ibidem Press, 2018). Her latest publication is a chapter on poetry for the *Routledge Companion to Literature and Disability*.

Rhys Feeney lives and teaches in Te Whanganui-a-Tara. His work has appeared in *Mimicry*, *Starling*, *elsewhere* and *Sponge*. His debut chapbook will appear as part of AUP *New Poets* in 2020.

Emma Gattey is a writer and critic from Ōtautahi. She is studying global and imperial history at Oxford University.

John Geraets edited the special issue on innovative writing of the *Journal of New Zealand Literature*. A selection of his own writing, *Everything is Something in Place*, was published by Titus Press in 2019.

Michael Giacon is a poet and songwriter from Auckland. This year he is a judge for the inaugural Peter Wells Short Fiction Contest.

Carolyn Gillum is a Winston Churchill McNeish Writer's Fellow. She won the Flash500 Novel Competition and was longlisted for the Bath Novel Award and Mslexia Novel Prize. Her work has been published in *The Spinoff*, *Headland* and *4th Floor Journal*, among others.

Star Gossage (Ngāti Wai/Ngāti Ruanui) lives and works surrounded by whānau on ancestral land at Pakiri, north of Auckland. Her emotionally intense paintings often feature dream-like tūpuna figures who seem imbued with collective memory. She is represented by Tim Melville Art Gallery in Auckland.

Patricia Grace is the author of seven novels, five short story collections and several children's books. She received the Prime Minister's Award for Literary Achievement in 2006 and was the recipient of the Neustadt International Prize for Literature sponsored by the University of Oklahoma in 2008. She was a recipient of the Distinguished Companion of the New Zealand Order of Merit in 2007, and received honorary doctorates for literature from Victoria University of Wellington (1989) and the World Indigenous Nations University (2016).

Eliana Gray is a poet from Ōtepoti. They like queer subtext in teen comedies and not much else. They have had words in *Sport*, *Mimicry*, *Minarets*, *Mayhem* and other publications. Their debut collection, *Eager to Break*, was published by Girls On Key Press (2019). This year they are undertaking residencies in Finland and Ōtepoti.

Isabel Haarhaus lives in Auckland with her family and is a writer and teacher. She has published short stories, poetry, essays and arts writing and is finishing a collection of linked short stories, *Other People's Houses*.

Bernadette Hall lives in Hurunui. In May 2020, Scythe Press will publish her YA novella, SUL, *an Antarctic Fable* with 22 new paintings by Dunedin artist Kathryn Madill.

Jordan Hamel is a Pōneke-based poet and performer. He grew up in Timaru on a healthy diet of Catholicism and masculine emotional repression. He was the 2018 New Zealand Poetry Slam champion and represented NZ at the World Poetry Slam Championships in the US. He has had work published in *Sport*, *takahē*, *Poetry New Zealand Yearbook*, *Mayhem*, *Mimicry*, *Queen Mob's Teahouse* and elsewhere.

Sarah Harpur has performed stand-up comedy at local and international fringe festivals, including the Edinburgh Fringe, and has an MA in scriptwriting from Victoria University of Wellington.

Jenna Heller is an award-winning writer who grew up in the US and now lives in Christchurch with her partner and their two children.

Stephanie Johnson is the author of 20 books: novels, poetry, short stories and non-fiction. She has also written for the screen and stage. In 2019 she published a novel *The Sisters' Lover* (as Lily Woodhouse), and a non-fiction/biography *West Island: Five twentieth-century New Zealanders in Australia* (Otago University Press).

Erik Kennedy is the author of *There's No Place Like the Internet in Springtime* (Victoria University Press, 2018), and he selected the poetry for *Queen Mob's Teahouse: The book* (Dostoyevsky Wannabe, 2019). He lives in Christchurch.

Brent Kininmont has lived in Tokyo for the past two decades. His first book of poems, *Thuds Underneath*, was published in 2015 by Victoria University Press.

Megan Kitching lives in Dunedin and tutors English and creative writing at the University of Otago. Her poetry has previously appeared in *The Frogmore Papers*, *Otago Daily Times*, *takahē* and *Landfall*.

Claire Lacey is the author of an award-winning book of poetry, *Twin Tongues*, and a graphic novel, *Selkie*. She is pursuing a PhD on brain injury and poetry at the University of Otago.

Leonard Lambert's most recent publication is a chapbook, *Winter Waves* (Cold Hub Press, 2018). He lives and paints in Napier.

Grace Lee is a writer and literature student from Auckland. She is currently an MPhil candidate at the University of Cambridge.

Wes Lee lives in Paekākāriki. Her latest poetry collection is *By the Lapels* (Steele Roberts, 2019). She has won a number of awards, including the BNZ Katherine Mansfield Literary Award. Most recently she was selected as a finalist for the Sarah Broom Poetry Prize 2018, and awarded the Poetry New Zealand Prize 2019 by Massey University Press.

Malinna Liang is the winner of every staring competition she has ever had with a baby, and a millennial, a foodie, a filmmaker and an aspiring writer. In that order.

Emer Lyons is from Cork and is a creative/critical PhD candidate in the English programme at the University of Otago. Her poetry, fiction and reviews have appeared in journals such as *The Stinging Fly*, *Poetry Ireland Review*, *The Tangerine*, *Headland*, *Mimicry*, *takahē*, *Southword*, *The Cardiff Review*, *London Grip* and *Queen Mob's Tea House*.

Owen Marshall, novelist, short story writer, poet and anthologist, has written or edited over 30 books. Awards include the Deutz Medal for Fiction, fellowships at Otago, Canterbury and Massey universities and the Katherine Mansfield Fellowship in France. He has been awarded the ONZM and the CNZM for services to literature and received the Prime Minister's Award for Literary Achievement. He is an adjunct professor at the University of Canterbury.

Talia Marshall (Ngāti Kuia/Rangitāne ō Wairau/Ngāti Rārua/Ngāti Takihiku) is the current Emerging Māori Writer in Residence at the IIML. Her first collection of poetry, *Bad Apple*, is forthcoming from Kilmog Press.

Carolyn McCurdie is a Dunedin writer. Her first collection of poetry was *Bones in the Octagon* (Mākaro Press, 2015). She is working on a second collection and a series of science fiction novels.

Poet and artist **Cilla McQueen** lives and works in the southern port of Bluff, Motupōhue. Her most recent poetry collection is *Poeta: Selected and new poems* (Otago University Press, 2018). Recently she and Adrienne Martyn exhibited 'Gossamer', a work of poetry and photography, at Mīharo, Invercargill.

Zoë Meager has a master's degree in creative writing from the University of Auckland, and her short stories have been published and commended at home and abroad. She is fiction editor for *takahē*.

James Norcliffe has published nine collections of poetry including *Shadow Play* (2013) and *Dark Days at the Oxygen Café* (2016). Recent work has appeared in *Acumen*, *The Cincinnati Review*, *Salamander*, *Gargoyle* and *Flash Fiction International* (Norton, 2015). With Michelle Elvy and Frankie McMillan he recently edited *Bonsai: Best small stories from Aotearoa New Zealand* (Canterbury University Press, 2018). He is a co-editor (with Michelle Elvy and Paula Morris) of *Ko Aotearoa Tātou* (forthcoming from Otago University Press).

Keith Nunes (Te Ika a Māui) was nominated for *Best Small Fictions* 2019, the Pushcart Prize, and has won the Flash Frontier Short Fiction Award. His poetry, short fiction and visuals have been published around the globe.

Kōtuku Titihuia Nuttall (Te Āti Awa, Ngāti Tūwharetoa, Ngāti Rangatahi, STÁ, UTW First Nation) is a writer and MA student from the Kāpiti Coast.

Vincent O'Sullivan's *Selected Short Stories* was published in 2019 and his novel *All This by Chance* in 2018 (both Victoria University Press). He lives in Dunedin.

Leanne Radojkovich's short story collection *First Fox* was published in 2017 by The Emma Press (UK). Most recently her stories have appeared in *Landfall 237*, *Lost Balloon* and *ReadingRoom*.

essa may ranapiri (Ngāti Wehi Wehi) is a poet from Kirikiriroa. Their poetry collection *ransack* was published by Victoria University Press in 2019. They will write until they're dead.

Gillian Roach graduated with a master's in creative writing from Auckland University of Technology in 2016. Gillian won the New Voices – Emerging Poets competition (2018) and was runner-up in the IWW Kathleen Grattan Prize for a Sequence of Poems in 2018 and 2019.

Pip Robertson lives in Wellington, and is getting back into writing short stories after years of writing things for other people and caring for a young family.

Jo-Ella Sarich is a lawyer, writer and mother of two living in Te Awa Kairangi. Her poems have appeared in a number of print and online publications, including the *New Statesman*, *The Lake*, *Cleaver*, *Barzakh*, *Quarterday Review*, *Shoreline of Infinity*, *takahē*, *Shot Glass Journal*, the New Zealand Poetry Society 2017 anthology, *After the Cyclone*, and *Poetry New Zealand Yearbook* 2017.

Tim Saunders farms sheep and beef near Palmerston North. He has had poetry and short stories published in *Turbine|Kapohau*, *takahē*, *NZ Listener* and *Flash Frontier*. He won the 2018 Mindfood Short Story Competition, and placed third in the 2019 National Flash Fiction Day awards. He performs poetry around the Manawatū region and beyond.

Sarah Scott was the winner of the 2019 New Voices – Emerging Poets prize. She has an MA in creative writing and her poems have been published in NZ journals such as *Landfall*, *Turbine|Kapohau* and *Up Country*. She lives in Wellington.

Sarah Shirley is a junior doctor working in Hamilton. Her poetry has appeared in *Landfall*, *takahē*, *Poetry New Zealand*, *Atlas*, *The Cider Press Review*, *Strange Horizons* and elsewhere.

Peter Simpson is a writer, editor and occasional curator who lives in Auckland. His recent publications include two volumes of the selected journals of Charles Brasch, *Volume Two: 1945–1957* and *Volume Three: 1958–1973* (Otago University Press, 2017 and 2018), and a two-volume study of Colin McCahon: *There is Only One Direction: Volume One, 1919–1959* and *Is This the Promised Land? Volume Two, 1960–1987* (Auckland University Press, 2019 and 2020). He received the Prime

Minister's Award for Literary Achievement (non-fiction) in 2017.

Elizabeth Smither's latest publications are *Night Horse* (Auckland University Press, 2017), which won the Ockham Poetry Award in 2018, and a novel, *Loving Sylvie* (Allen & Unwin, 2019).

Charlotte Steel works as an instructional designer in Dunedin. She likes to count hawks while driving around Central Otago. Her work has previously been accepted by *Starling*, *Re-Draft*, *IKA* and *Mayhem*

Nicola Thorstensen is a Dunedin-based writer and a member of the Octagon Poetry Collective, which organises monthly poetry readings. Her work has appeared recently in *Ngā Kupu Waikato: An anthology of Waikato poetry*.

Rushi Vyas lives in Ōtepoti/Dunedin. Originally from the US, his first full-length poetry manuscript was a finalist in the National Poetry Series (US) in 2018 and 2019.

Susan Wardell lives in Dunedin, where she lectures in social anthropology while raising two small humans and a variety of green things. Her poetry has appeared in a number of publications in Australia and NZ. She placed second in the 2018 Landfall Essay Competition.

Robert West lives in Dunedin. His work focuses on the ways in which people and things, organic or manmade, interconnect: neural pathways, children's games, GIS mapping, cellular structures. His work is represented by Moray Gallery, Dunedin.

CONTRIBUTIONS
Landfall publishes original poems, essays, short stories, excerpts from works of fiction and non-fiction in progress, reviews, articles on the arts, and portfolios by artists. Submissions must be emailed to landfall@otago.ac.nz with 'Landfall submission' in the subject line.

Visit our website www.otago.ac.nz/press/landfall/index.html for further information.

SUBSCRIPTIONS
Landfall is published in May and November. The subscription rates for 2020 (two issues) are: New Zealand $55 (including GST); Australia $NZ65; rest of the world $NZ70. Sustaining subscriptions help to support New Zealand's longest running journal of arts and letters, and the writers and artists it showcases. These are in two categories: Friend: between $NZ75 and $NZ125 per year. Patron: $NZ250 and above.

Send subscriptions to Otago University Press, PO Box 56, Dunedin, New Zealand. For enquiries, email landfall@otago.ac.nz or call 64 3 479 8807.

Print ISBN: 978-1-98-859243-5
ePDF ISBN: 978-1-98-859244-2
ISSN 00–23–7930

Published by Otago University Press, 533 Castle Street, Dunedin, New Zealand.

Typeset by Otago University Press.
Printed in New Zealand by Caxton.

creative nz
Arts Council of New Zealand Toi Aotearoa

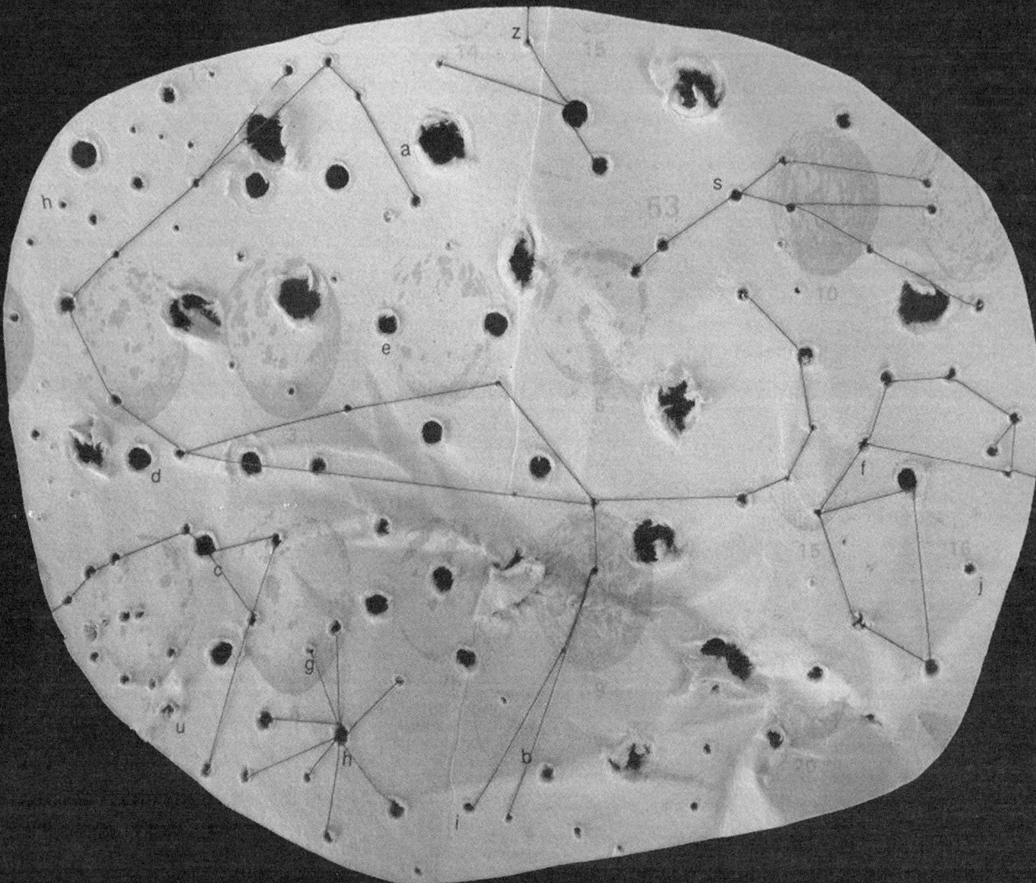

Robert West, Untitled, silkscreen, cotton and letraset on paper, 240 x 185mm.